Praise For Woodworking Business: Start Quickly and Operate Successfully

Woodworking Business: Start Quickly and Operate Successfully is a must read with practical tips on every aspect of the woodworking trade. I would recommend this book to anyone in the woodworking profession. The insight within this book will do wonders for your business. It is one of the few books I have read more than once. This book is a remarkable tool that not only helped me in the beginning; it serves as a reference that I can look back on when I have questions about my business.

Chris Looney
Hardwood Technology
http://hardwoodtechnology.com

I would like to thank you for your latest book Woodworking Business: Start Quickly and Operate Successfully. It has been of immense value to me while I start up my own woodworking business. I soon discovered that it is an entire business plan and that alone has saved me hundreds of hours of writing and research. I particularly liked your simplified woodworking chapter which I intend to adopt to improve my profitability. Thank you again.

Neil Rogers
Neil Rogers Woodcraft
Beaconsfield, Tasmania, Australia

This book's purpose is to help the reader make money from woodworking skills. The advice and information are true to that purpose. The writer's voice is clear, trustworthy, and human, and the italicized personal stories are great. All told, a wealth of relevant and useful guidance.

Sandy M.
Austin, TX

Woodworking Business:
Start Quickly And Operate Successfully

**An Expert Woodworker Reveals
The Keys To Succeeding
In The Woodworking Business**

A. William Benitez

Woodworking Business:
Start Quickly And Operate Successfully

An Expert Woodworker Reveals
The Keys To Succeeding
In The Woodworking Business

A. William Benitez

Published By
Positive Imaging, LLC
9016 Palace Parkway
Austin, TX 78748

Cover design by A. William Benitez. Cover photo by Sandy M.

ISBN 978-0-9842480-3-2

Dedication

To my wife Barbara Frances, the love of my life, for her creative spirit, invaluable advice, and steadfast support with every project I undertake. As the years pass she is always there to help me continue growing.

Contents

Introduction

Woodworking is a truly enjoyable hobby for thousands of men and women around the world. It provides a unique opportunity to hand craft wood projects for family members, friends, and yourself. For many men and women it's also a lucrative full or part-time business. They use their skills to make a living or enhance the income from a job. Your investment in this book reflects a strong interest in following their example. With woodworking you can make extra money or even a good living doing work you love.

Whether you're an experienced woodworker who has built many projects over the years, or an advanced amateur honing your skills, this book can help you make money with woodworking. You may already be using those skills to make money on a part-time basis. Some of you may even have your own small woodworking business and simply want to increase your profits. If you have woodworking skills, this book could help you to profit from them.

The information contained here can guide you in building a successful one-person woodworking business. It's not intended as information for developing a corporation to market wood products on a large-scale. There may be other books that address that subject, but the emphasis of this book is the one-person business.

As an avid woodworker, it may seem odd to you that the first step is to ask if you are absolutely certain that operating a woodworking business is really what you want to do. This is an important question because woodworking as a hobby, just for the enjoyment, is not the same as running a woodworking business.

Actually, the considerations are the same for any small business because it involves a lot of work. It's definitely not the same as a job where you work for someone else. Take the time to think about it carefully before transitioning from hobbyist to professional woodworker. This is the first step because it's critically important and the first chapter will help you make those determinations so you can avoid beginning something that isn't right for you.

Once you are certain it's the right choice, the next step is an in-depth inventory of all your skills. During this inventory you want to determine the skills you believe have the most value to others.

Remember that different people have varying skills and various levels of those skills. To do the best possible work and ensure profit for yourself and the satisfaction of your customers, you need to recognize the things you do best and the weaker areas where improvement is necessary. Chapter two will help you to discover your best skills and show you how to make the best possible use of them while helping you develop others.

Tools

Woodworking requires a significant collection of highly functional tools. However, it's not necessary that all of them be commercial-duty when getting started. If you have already been building projects, your present collection of tools may be adequate for most work. Chapters three, four, and five will describe the tools you need, help you make the best use of the tools you already have, explain ways to improve the effectiveness of the less costly consumer-level tools, and offer some guidance for buying new tools.

Shop Space

It is definitely best to have a shop space to build woodworking projects. Even so, there are some woodworkers who build various projects on site and take advantage of the space that customers have available by setting up their tools on site. Most often they set up in a garage or storage building. Chapter six describes what kind of space works well for the woodworking business and how best to organize your shop. It also discusses conducting a woodworking business without significant shop space and the difficulties this may cause for your business.

Licensing, Accounting, And Taxes

Once your inventories are complete and you have a functional shop space, it's almost time to really get started with the business of woodworking. Before contacting your first potential customer, take care of your licensing, accounting, and income taxes. These areas, especially income taxes, have consistently created problems for small business owners and chapter seven will help you deal with all three.

First, it encourages you to determine and adhere to the small business requirements of your community. Then it helps you to handle all the accounting necessary for a successful business. Finally, it guides you in meeting those all important IRS requirements.

Getting Started

Then it's time to start that most important step of making your business visible to as many people as possible. To succeed, businesses need customers and chapter eight helps you with marketing and advertising methods that will bring in customers while keeping costs down.

Another much overlooked aspect of business covered in this chapter is the critically important topic of keeping customers. This can never be overemphasized because it costs much more to get new customers than to keep the ones you have.

Setting Prices

To succeed you must know how much to charge for every job. This is a seemingly complex topic in the woodworking business as it is in other businesses. There is good reason to get it right because charging too much will almost certainly cause you to lose jobs to lower bidders. On the other hand, charging too little could cause you to lose money. Neither of these is an attractive option because either way your business will suffer.

In chapter nine you will find a concise method for calculating how much to charge for every job. To check your figures and make certain you will make money, there is also a solid secondary method for carefully checking the accuracy of your pricing before you commit to an under-priced job.

In time, your experience, reputation, and level of expertise will increase and your prices need to rise accordingly. This chapter will help you determine the best time to raise your prices so you can always get the highest possible amount for your work.

Contracting Jobs

You may be thinking that how much you get paid is the most important thing but it's even more critical to get paid in full for every job. Don't take for granted that customers will pay you. Ensure full payment by using the solid and consistent contracting and collection methods described clearly in chapter ten.

In addition to the clear and concise instructions, you will find copies of useful forms and direct links to forms that you can easily download and edit to use for your business so you won't have to spend a lot of time creating forms.

Getting Help

This book is based entirely on first-hand experience operating a one-person woodworking business. Most woodworkers prefer doing things on their own and aren't interested in adding the complexities and problems of dealing with employees and payroll to their small business. Nevertheless, there may be times when you need help to deliver and install jobs or to complete certain jobs to meet deadlines.

Chapter eleven covers how to deal with these issues by using subcontractors or other individuals to assist you without violating IRS regulations and running into payroll deduction or Social Security issues.

Simplifying While Maintaining Quality

Many woodworkers enjoy using traditional woodworking methods to ensure quality work. This is certainly one way to build projects but not the only way. There are simpler methods and in chapter twelve you are asked to consider such methods to help you work faster and increase profits. None of these methods reduce the quality of the work but they do facilitate faster completion and often increase profits. Read this with an open mind and then make your own decisions about how best to make use of the information.

The main goal of this book is to help you profit from your existing skills, not to teach you woodworking. Nevertheless, no matter your skill level, there is always much more to learn. With that in mind, the simplified methods included were gleaned over many years in business. Applying these methods could help you deliver quality work quickly and will definitely contribute to a higher profit margin.

Chapter twelve has information on all these simplified methods in hopes that you also will find them of value. This information is not a criticism of traditional methods or any methods you already use. Simplified methods are presented solely in the interest of increasing your income from woodworking activities.

This book was written for woodworkers who have sufficient skills to build projects or at least the capacity to learn how to build them. It is assumed that you already have a sufficiently high level of woodworking skills to complete some projects in return for fair payment.

Safety

Chapter thirteen is the most critical in this entire book because it is about safety. Woodworking can be dangerous because it involves the use of power tools that can cause serious injury if used carelessly or without full attention. This chapter includes information to help you avoid injuries throughout your woodworking career. Please take the time to read this information carefully and take it to heart. If you carefully adhere to these basic rules they will help you avoid injuries that can ruin your business and perhaps your entire life.

The Order Of Things

The basic message of chapter fourteen is "Think!" Keep your mind on your work and open to new ways. Always think about what you are doing. Take the time to do things in the best possible order to make certain you are measuring correctly, carrying out your own plans, and remaining safe.

Woodworking requires assembly of projects and while it may seem trivial to some, the order of assembly often makes a significant difference in quality. This chapter will help you to stay fully attentive to your work to ensure quality and safety.

Everyday Lessons

In chapter fifteen there is a collection of valuable lessons about real jobs that were done over the years. In addition to many details about the jobs, there are drawings and photographs that will help you to understand exactly what was done and how it was handled. This chapter is filled with examples of jobs that could well be similar to those you will be doing.

Final Notes

The last chapter includes a valuable collection of notes compiled over many years while dealing with customers and working on projects. Some of these will help you do a better job or make jobs easier. In chapter sixteen many of these ideas are explored in detail. They are called final notes because they were added to the book to share valuable details that have continued to be gleaned over the years. These ideas may be helpful to you while starting and operating your woodworking business.

One

Is Being A Small Business Owner For You?

The answer to this question may seem obvious since you just purchased a woodworking business guide. Actually, it really isn't easy to answer accurately. Nevertheless, it is critical to answer this question honestly now, before committing yourself to starting any business, including woodworking.

Your purchase of this book illustrates a real interest in starting and operating a woodworking business. That's a good start but, more importantly, you should be certain you are suited to operating a small business. You don't want to put in the effort and investment of time and money only to find that the woodworking business is not for you.

Small Business Ownership

Do you really know what is involved in owning and operating a one-person small business? You need to know because it differs from other forms of small business. Most likely, you will be the sole owner, boss, designer, accountant, receptionist, salesperson, cabinetmaker, and cleanup person. You may have a relative or close friend to help you with some of the work but all the responsibility rests with you. All problems, simple or complex, are yours to handle. Prospects, customers, vendors, and everyone else will look to you for answers. Are you up for that? Now is the time to decide.

Unlike the consistent flow of problems, your income will come in spurts, usually upon completion and installation of a project. If the project is delayed, so is the payment but the bills continue coming in like clock work.

If you get sick, everything stops, especially the income. For health care insurance, a high cost item, you're on your own. Whenever you take a day off or even go on a long and much-needed vacation, everything comes to a halt, including the money.

You are the sole contact for your customers, so expect calls at strange hours. Whenever a problem comes up, you are the one they will call. No one else is responsible so all complaints come directly to you. Regardless of how good you are and how well you do the work, problems will arise and customers will turn to you. Running a one-person woodworking business takes patience, caring, understanding, and lots of time to deal with all the problems to satisfy your customers.

Since time is money in any business, being well organized is essential. Much of your work will involve dealing with existing jobs but prospects will be contacting you to request information and quotes on new jobs. This is also an important aspect of your work since the work must continue to flow. Many times you will have to leave important work unfinished to handle these sales calls. After you visit these prospects you will probably need to do some design work, calculate job costs, and prepare contracts and specifications. It's a lot of work and you are the one that has to do it all.

Suitability For Small Business Ownership

I like to illustrate how being unsuited for running a small business can create problems with a story about a friend of mine. He is a highly competent woodworker who works for a large kitchen cabinet manufacturer and has been with them for many years.

Years ago he decided that he wanted to own and operate his own woodworking business and he was quite serious. He was tired of using his talents to make money for someone else. He set up his garage as a woodworking shop and began purchasing and setting up all the tools he needed. It took him a long time because he insisted on purchasing only commercial-duty tools and the costs were quite high. After about a year of preparations and saving some money to tide him over while he built his business, he quit his job and got started in earnest.

He had a large family and many friends so jobs began coming in quickly. It seemed like everything was going to work out great for him as he quickly developed a backlog of woodworking projects. Unfortunately, something changed when he started working for himself and it was interesting to watch.

After years of arriving at work on time everyday and working long hours on his job, it seemed as if he lost that discipline. He began sleeping in, sometimes until nearly noon. Then he would often work just a few hours and take off. He would close the shop and hang out with friends.

He and his friends would go fishing, drive around, or simply hang around together. Sometimes he wouldn't open the shop for days at a time so not only did his work get delayed but he missed calls from potential customers as this was before cell phones were a popular part of everyday life.

Soon he was missing deadlines and customers began complaining. Even his friends stopped recommending him and his income slowly came to a halt. The few customers whose jobs he finally finished certainly would not recommend him to others.

It wasn't long before he closed his woodworking business and went back to work for his previous employer who happily took him back and he immediately went back to his highly disciplined schedule.

I had great respect for his woodworking skills and believed he would succeed easily but it was obvious that he lacked the self motivation and discipline essential for running a small business. As a self-motivated person I couldn't understand why he could keep a perfect schedule and work so hard for someone else but not for himself. It became clear that he was not self-motivated. He had the discipline but he needed someone to provide the motivation for performing tasks promptly and competently. When there was no one else to control things, he was unable to motivate himself to run a small business successfully.

Please don't think that this is intended as a criticism of my friend or to discourage you from starting your own woodworking business. Some people are best suited to being good employees. There is absolutely nothing wrong with that. Some of us are sufficiently self-motivated to run a small business. I ran a woodworking business for more than 20 years before retiring from it and found it enjoyable and challenging. Perhaps you can do the same.

An Accurate Picture

This chapter offers an accurate picture of what it takes to run your own small business successfully. While the goal of this book is to help you start and operate your own successful woodworking business, you won't find any hype about the romance of running such a business. You need to see all the warts because it's not easy and it takes a significant effort to succeed financially.

There are some who would paint the woodworking business and any other small business as a simple way to make lots of money by being your own boss and not doing much work. That's an inaccurate picture of what it takes to succeed.

Now you have an important decision to make and if you choose to start a woodworking business this book will help you every step of the way. If after reading this chapter you are still certain that a woodworking business is what you want, then go ahead without hesitation because now have a clear picture of what it takes to succeed.

—

Two

Inventory Of Your Skills

Exploring All The Possibilities

Woodworking may involve many different kinds of work in addition to building furniture and cabinets. It can also include the repair of cabinets and furniture, the installation of doors and various kinds of moldings, and wood repairs, just to name a few. What are your specific skills? What kind of work have you done regularly over the years? Make a list of the jobs you consider your forte. These are the skills to market immediately. This will probably involve work that you have already done for yourself, family members, or friends. You already have the practice necessary for these jobs so you will do them well for your new customers.

Next, create a list of the kind of work you want to do; work that you would love to be doing. It could be building entertainment centers or perhaps kitchen cabinets. There is probably a specific kind of project that you really enjoy and other people appreciate. Add this kind of project to your list. Once you have created that list, determine your level of competence in each of those jobs. For some you may feel competent so add them to the list of forte items. For others you may need some improvement and you can practice that kind of work before doing it for customers. It is important to handle the work competently before you begin selling it to customers. Unless you are fully confident that you can deliver a good job, avoid that kind of work when you are starting your business.

Learning and Training

Once you decide the areas where you need training, start by reading all you can about that kind of work. Search the web or look through woodworking books you already own. Purchase books with helpful related information. Check out the work of others and see what they do and how they do it. You may not follow their methods exactly but it will give you ideas for developing your own methods.

Once you have a handle on how to do it, practice by creating something for your home, for a friend, or for a family member. Or, design something and build it and if it turns out great, sell it to someone to make up the cost of materials. If you do it for yourself there is a double benefit. Not only do you improve your skills for the future but you also gain furniture or repairs for your home or office. You can also photograph the pieces for use in an album or web site to advertise your work.

Handyman Skills

Don't overlook handyman skills. If you regularly repair things around your home, you could do the same for customers. You could even develop part of your business doing repairs on rental properties. This kind of work can be quite lucrative because it involves mostly small jobs that can be finished and collected for quickly.

> *Even though ninety percent of my work involved furniture and cabinets, I still accepted lucrative repair jobs. For several years I did repair work on rental properties owned by one person. Originally, he had called me from a small ad I placed in one of the weekly newspapers in my area. After a few jobs he began to call me regularly. Sometimes it took me away from the cabinet work that I preferred but it was quite lucrative. During one year his jobs totaled over $13,000.00. Not bad from only one customer.*

Door Work

Doors are a consistent problem in homes. Foundations settle and doors begin to stick at the top or the bottom. Or, the space between the door and the jamb might tighten up and cause the door to get stuck or open up and allow heat or cold to pass. If you have skills in this area, it can be lucrative. This can also include replacing doors. It's important to know what you are doing when replacing doors. This is especially true when installing an expensive exterior door. You don't want to ruin an expensive door because of inadequate skills.

> *My father was a general contractor and I was born into construction. By the time I graduated from high school I could build a house from the ground up but door work was my forte. I could hang doors from scratch faster than most of my contemporaries and could diagnose and correct door problems easily. When I started my woodworking business I advertised for door work even before I had my shop ready to go. I got many small jobs that kept the money flowing while I finished setting up my shop.*

Your Strongest Skills

What is your strongest skill and how can you use it to full advantage? Answer that question and start profiting from your woodworking business almost immediately. Here are a few other examples of how to take advantage of your best skills.

You may have already built some furniture for friends and family. If they liked the furniture, it should be obvious that you have skills in this area. Why not advertise for furniture projects right away. You know that you can do the work and you have completed projects that you can photograph to prove your abilities.

If you built furniture, you can certainly repair furniture. These skills also lend themselves to building and repairing kitchen cabinets. Your furniture skills will extend to many areas. Have your furniture projects included some woodcarving? If so, you can advertise to antique shops for carving repair work. They sometimes need small parts carved for expensive pieces.

Even if you start by specializing in a certain kind of work, that doesn't stop you from accepting other jobs. Always remain open to considering other work even as you try to stick with your strongest skills during the first year. This helps you maintain a good comfort level while still making a good profit and learning new things. This strikes a good balance that will help you succeed quickly if you just remember to avoid accepting jobs that make you feel uncomfortable because of limited skills.

> *On more than one occasion I have been called to help a woodworker finish a project that was beyond his skills. Sometimes I could help finish it but other times the design was so poor that it was necessary to start from scratch. You don't want that to happen anytime, much less during your first year. Not only will it cost you one or more customers, but it will also be a blow to your confidence.*

Study To Keep Learning

Study the woodworking craft to improve your skills. Read everything you can find about building the kinds of projects that interest you most. Don't just use the project plans, study them carefully to learn from them. Go to furniture stores and study the various methods they use to assemble cabinets. They use simpler methods and you want to learn to work as simply as possible. Once you have learned enough from both sources use the information to create your own methods that are simpler yet allow you to use the tools you have available and work faster.

Be Creative

No matter what methods you use, work at being creative. Make changes to the ideas you develop. Be original and your work will have its own identity and higher value. There are many woodworkers who build projects using the instructions and drawings directly from magazines or some other source. There is nothing wrong with that but it's best to change and improve the designs. There are many good designs that can be changed to make them your own. Most clients appreciate originality and, more importantly, they are usually willing to pay more for it.

What Size Jobs Should You Take?

Beyond just your skill level, it's also important to decide the size of jobs you will accept. Running a one person business requires that you be able to do jobs alone. If a job seems too big, chances are it will be a problem for you at that particular time. Perhaps later, when you have acquired more experience, you might consider those bigger jobs.

> *I would always figure what I could do alone and that would be all that I would accept. I did consider larger jobs but only if I felt confident that I could finish them in a reasonable time and without hiring help. During the first year stick to what you know you can do and then grow slowly as your skills increase.*

Three

Inventory Of Your Tools

You May Have The Tools You Need To Start

If you have already built cabinets and/or furniture, you know it takes a reasonably large collection of power and hand tools to do a good job. To be successful in the woodworking business requires having all the tools needed to complete the jobs you contract.

Most of you know that you need sufficient tools to do the jobs you contract but not everyone does. Recently, while building new cabinets for our kitchen, I hired an electrician to move some duplex receptacles to a new location. He arrived with a helper and promptly asked to borrow a screwdriver and a pair of pliers. My first instinct was to just send him away because of this obvious lack of professionalism. Since I needed the job done quickly to go ahead with the cabinet installation, I thought better of it and let him complete the job. Would you call him back for another job? It's doubtful that I will. Professionals have all the tools needed for the job and that is what you need to do to succeed financially in the woodworking business.

The best way to decide if you have what you need is with an inventory of all the tools you already own. Do you have a complete shop in your garage? Do you already have all the tools you need to build projects for your family and friends? If so, you are well ahead of the game because the same tools you have used will serve your business. You are ready to start getting paid for your work.

If you aren't certain that you have everything you need, this chapter and the next two include lists and details about most of the tools normally required for a woodworking business.

The table saw and related power tools, like the radial arm saw and/or sliding compound miter saw, are critical to any woodworking shop. These are the tools used to cut all the materials needed for most projects. Because of the importance of the table saw and other ripping and crosscutting equipment, all of chapter four is devoted to complete details about those tools. This chapter deals with the other power tools that are useful in a woodworking shop. Chapter five includes complete information about the hand tools useful for woodworking.

Purchasing Power Tools

You can find many of the power tools you need at local home improvement stores. There are also many companies who specialize in selling quality, trade-level tools to persons in the various trades. These are the best places to buy tools for the woodworking business, if your budget allows.

Don't overlook the many online stores that sell tools of all kinds. You may be able to save money by shopping for tools on the Internet. The best way to buy on the Internet is to start by checking out what you want at the local stores. When buying tools it always helps to see them first hand and even hold them in your hands. Take the time to make certain the tool has the features you need. Then get the make and model number and check the Internet to find out if any special prices are available on the models you want. Remember to take into account the price of shipping. Also consider that many companies will not charge sales tax if their company does not have a presence in your state.

Stationary Power Tools

This is a list of the stationary tools most commonly used by woodworkers. It is not a complete list and you may need other stationary
power tools. If your work requires such tools, you should definitely
buy them. Otherwise, I suggest you make do with the power tools
listed below.

The Band Saw

The band saw is a useful tool for many projects. It is especially well
suited to cutting curves in wood but, depending on the blade used, it
can do many other tasks including cutting tenons, if you use mortise
and tenon joinery. The size you need will be directly related to the
kind of work you will be doing. The ideal band saw has a fourteen-
inch depth of cut and a fourteen-inch throat so you can make almost
any cut.

For those with a tight budget there are many smaller units that perform adequately for many tasks. A good choice would be six-inch
depth of cut band saw with a twelve to fourteen-inch throat. This
would probably serve you well for many years and the cost will be
much lower that the larger unit. In addition, you can find models
that have optional risers to facilitate a twelve inch depth of cut for
thicker materials.

The Drill Press

Next on the list is the drill press. Accurate drilling requires a drill
press. While a large, floor mounted drill press is nice to have, a
smaller tabletop unit will serve just as well for most projects. It is
important to place a tabletop drill press on a strong and steady work
surface and fasten it securely to the tabletop using lag screws or
bolts.

For many jobs it 's useful to cut a piece of plywood about twelve inches by thirty inches and fasten it with lag bolts to the metal table of the drill press. This small wood surface serves as an excellent place to fasten various useful jigs and fences to help in the performance of various drilling tasks.

> *I am an avid fan of the concealed European hinges such as those made by the Blum company. The drill press with the tabletop described above is an excellent tool for drilling the thirty-five millimeter diameter holes required for these hinges. Of course, you can invest in a specialized drill and insertion setup but it is quite costly and a good drill press setup, even with an inexpensive drill press, will do the job. I used European hinges for years with this exact arrangement and never felt the need to invest in the specialized units. By setting up a good adjustable fence with small clamps I could drill the doors quickly and accurately for all my jobs. For those unfamiliar with these hinges, which have many helpful adjustments, the online stores that sell them have excellent reference material available at no cost. Use this valuable information to ensure a good installation.*

The Thickness Planer

A thickness planer can be an invaluable tool for anyone working with hardwoods. The hardwood you find in home improvement stores is already fully planed and considerably more expensive. It's best to find a local hardwood store that caters to professional furniture and cabinet makers so you can buy rough or rough planed hardwood for a lower price.

These stores are sometimes known as forest products stores. They often carry an extensive selection of sheet goods and hardwoods. Some of them also carry related cabinet hardware such as various kinds of hinges and drawer glides. Purchasing from these stores affords you much more control over the final quality of the hardwood surfaces. This requires knowledge of how best to select and work with hardwoods. You may already have this knowledge, otherwise you can learn about it from many excellent books and on the Internet including many valuable videos on YouTube. Just do a search for woodworking information and instructions. Follow up this research with some practice of the techniques.

If you have the room and the funds to invest in one, a large commercial planer does an excellent job. They are expensive and difficult to move around. For most work, a good twelve-inch portable thickness planer will serve you well for preparing hardwood boards for your projects. In a small shop these portable units make the most sense.

Thickness planers, even small models, are stationary tools and they should be bolted down to a strong, flat surface for use. You can use it as a portable unit but always fasten it down before turning it on. In addition to the possible movement because of the motor running, as long boards are run through they could affect the balance of the machine during a moment of inattention.

Belt and Disc Combination Sanders

The combination belt and disc sander is another valuable stationary power tool. These units are available in two basic sizes. The smaller one, that is readily available at any home improvement store, is the four-inch wide belt with six-inch disc model. This will work reasonably well but the work you can do is limited by its small size.

The larger unit with the six- inch wide belt and the eight or ten-inch disc makes it easier to sand larger pieces and the larger surface facilitates keeping your work piece aligned for a better sanding job. The wider belt also facilitates sanding several small pieces at once and this can save you a great deal of time when working on smaller projects. These larger units also have heavier duty motors and structures so they hold up under heavy duty use.

The Router

Routers are useful for many projects and they are included with the list of stationary tools because they can be used either as a portable power tool or stationary with a router table. While lightweight, consumer grade routers are adequate, I strongly urge you to buy a heavier unit that will accommodate both ¼ and ½-inch shank router bits. This way you can make use of any bits you already have but then buy the better and stronger ½-inch shank bits in the future.

With the router you should buy or build a good, solid router table. It need not be large but it is essential that it be stable. There are many router procedures that are made easier and safer with the router fastened upside down to a table. It's an important and easy-to-use accessory that increases the value of your router. Placing your router in this arrangement converts it to an excellent stationary tool.

Routers are invaluable for many tasks including cutting dados, rabbets, and many decorative edges. In addition to the router table, there are many other accessories that allow you to perform many tasks including cutting circles.

Portable Power Tools

In addition to stationary power tools, there are many portable power tools that are useful in most woodworking shops. These include the biscuit joiner, drill, circular saw, saber saw (jig saw), reciprocal saw (cut saw), rotary saw (zip saw), and the handheld planer, to name just a few. If you already have all of these, you are ready to use them on jobs as they come in. Otherwise, I suggest that you buy them as the need arises for a specific job. This way you can assign the cost of the purchase to the job and avoid spending a great deal out-of-pocket before jobs come in.

The Plate or Biscuit Joiner

A plate (biscuit) joiner can be an invaluable addition to any shop. This is a tool that will simplify your joinery while still providing strong and attractive joints. While biscuit joinery is not the equal of well executed mortise and tenon or dovetail joinery, the wafers used with plate joinery provide a strong and easier to align alternative to more complex joinery and it ensures strong joints using simpler and faster methods. In those cases where the joinery itself is not visible as part of the design, plate joinery serves as an excellent substitute.

Quality furniture often requires complex and time-consuming joinery. This is sometimes replaced by using dowels that are a poor substitute for good joinery techniques. The wafers used in biscuit joinery are easier to align while the glue is drying and provide a stronger joint than dowels because they have over twenty times the glue surface.

I began using a biscuit joiner many years ago when I saw one at a tile and plastic laminate store. I was fascinated with the possibilities and purchased it on the spot. It turned out to be an excellent investment that served me well for many years.

Over the years I discussed the biscuit joiner with many woodworkers and realized that some of them feel that it compromises what they consider good joinery. I never argue with these woodworkers since they certainly have a right to work in any way they choose. Nor is my choice of the biscuit joiner a criticism of traditional joinery.

My intent in this book is to help woodworkers profit from their skills with proven methods that worked for me over many years. Use of the biscuit joiner is a part of these methods. I sincerely believe it helped me to work faster while still delivering a quality product. If you believe that the only way to deliver a quality product is using traditional joinery methods, then that is exactly what you should do.

Like the biscuit joiner, it was obvious that there were other tools that seemed to cause controversy with some woodworkers. One of those tools is the pneumatic nailer. Some woodworkers are insulted by the idea of using nails in any form, much less with a power nailer.

The Pneumatic Nailer: A Controversial Time Saver

Some woodworkers frown on the use of nails to build cabinets. Traditional joinery is an excellent way to assemble cabinets but it isn't the only way. For years I've used pneumatic finish nailers for cabinet assembly. These nailers have saved me many hours and do an adequate job. As one example, I assemble kitchen cabinets using a plate joiner. Instead of waiting for the glue to dry while a cabinet is clamped up, I use a few nails to hold the units together while they dry. Most of these nails are between the cabinet units and not visible when the cabinets are installed. In addition to saving time it saves me the cost of clamps and the time of waiting for units to dry so I can reuse the clamps.

In some cabinets you can even use the nails where they are visible. Not all jobs involve elegant furniture or cabinets. In addition, many of my jobs were laminate clad so that all the nails were covered up by the plastic laminate. Using a pneumatic nailer reduced my assembly time and increased my profits. For those who value profit and quality, this is an invaluable tool.

To some, screws are somewhat controversial but I have found them invaluable for many of my jobs. Not every job is an heirloom. Actually, probably very few of your jobs will fall into that category. There will be many customers for whom *price is an important concern and over the years I was able to serve many of them because of my use of these techniques.*

The Drill

Portable drills are an important tool in any shop. While it is convenient to use battery operated power drills, a standard electric drill will work well in a shop environment and avoids the need to continuously charge the batteries. Nevertheless, the portability and lack of electrical cords on the floor makes battery-powered drills attractive to many. Should you choose to use a battery-powered model make certain you buy a unit with at least two batteries to avoid delaying a job while waiting for a battery to fully charge.

The Circular Saw

This is really a carpenter's tool but woodworkers can find it a handy power tool for certain kinds of work. While many carpenters use the circular saw in a freehand fashion, that is seldom useful while building woodworking projects. But used in conjunction with a rip or crosscut guide it can be a useful tool. You can buy a rip guide or create rip and crosscut guides using plywood to make it an accurate saw. (See pages 49 to 51 for details about making your own guides.)

The Saber Saw (Jig Saw)

This is an invaluable tool for cutting curves and circles and also for cutouts in cabinets. There are many extremely cheap models available and they should be avoided because they cut poorly and are subject to excessive vibration that impedes accuracy. Invest in a well made, name brand, unit that will handle all the jobs that come along. These units are more costly and usually include variable speeds and an orbital action setting for the blade that facilitates much faster and more accurate cutting.

It is a good idea to also have a good set of blades for rough and fine cutting. Blades with larger teeth cut faster but rougher than blades with smaller teeth which are best for fine cuts. For cutting through surfaces with plastic laminate, blades with the teeth pointing down are available to avoid tear out of the laminate while cutting.

The Reciprocal Saw (Cut Saw)

This is a saw that you may not use much but when needed there is nothing that can take its place. Making cutouts in a wall or the side of a cabinet is made much easier with this saw. If you don't already own one, wait until you get a job where it is a necessary tool before purchasing one. Then invest in a good one and it will last you for many years and do a good job for you when needed.

The Rotary Saw (Zip Saw)

This small tool is similar to a small router or trimmer and uses specialized bits that not only drill through a surface but also cut in a line. It is useful for cutting holes in cabinets to accommodate electrical receptacles and pipes or holes in almost any surface for other purposes. It is an especially useful tool for cabinet installations.

The Portable Electric Planer

There are times when the only way to smooth out the edge of material is with a portable planer. It is an excellent tool for door installations but can also serve an important function in a woodworking shop. If you don't already have one, don't invest in it until you have a job where it will be of real value to you. You can definitely function without one of these machines.

Carbide Tipped Blades and Bits

Whether you purchase trade-level or consumer-level tools, invest in carbide tipped blades and bits. Most new power saws now bring carbide tipped blades but these are inexpensive blades with a small number of teeth. Fine woodwork requires a high quality blade with at least forty teeth and in many cases sixty or eighty teeth. This will give you a much finer cut thereby improving the overall quality of your work. Whether purchasing power saw blades or router bits, insist on carbide tipped edges. High speed steel edges require constant, time-consuming, sharpening to deliver a smooth cut.

While carbide tipped blades and bits don't require sharpening often, they must be sharpened if used regularly. Find a company to handle this for you. It is difficult and time-consuming to do a good sharpening job on carbide edges without the proper tools. Just be sure to keep all your blades and bits sharp and ready to use to avoid delays in completing jobs and damage to wood surfaces.

Four

Ripping And Crosscutting Power Saws

Using sheet goods such as plywood, particle board, and fiberboard is common in woodworking businesses. Ripping and crosscutting these sheets can be cumbersome and requires specialized power tools and accessories. These include the table saw, radial arm saw, and the sliding compound miter saw.

Table Saw

The table saw is normally the heart of a woodworking shop and with accessories can be used to cut almost every project even if it isn't the best tool for some cuts. There are several familiar brands including Ryobi, Ridgid, Delta, Makita, Grizzly, Jet, and others. Don't avoid a brand simply because it isn't listed here. Just try to buy one that will allow you to do precision work without breaking your budget.

Commercial-duty models are expensive but are definitely rock solid, accurate, and almost devoid of vibration. Nevertheless, they are not essential for the everyday work of most woodworkers. Buy one that you can afford and fits the size of your space while remembering you are investing in one of the most important tools in your shop.

Keep the table saw you have unless it is one of those $99.00, light weight, specials. The main problem with these light weight, inexpensive table saws is the high level of vibration and limited accuracy. While difficult and unwise, you can produce reasonably good work even with one of these inexpensive saws.

When I retired from the woodworking business I sold the major power tools including a commercial-duty table saw. My plans were to build a small shop behind the house so I could build projects for myself, not for business purposes. Before I completed the shop it became obvious that we needed new office furniture for our home office. I still had most of the tools that I needed but not a table saw. Since I had no place to keep a large saw I decided to buy one of those $99.00 units.

To reduce vibration and increase accuracy, I built a four-foot by eight-foot table using a sheet of ¾-inch plywood framed with 2X4 lumber. Instead of using the flimsy legs that came with the saw, I cut out the table to accommodate it and screwed it in place. I also constructed a four-foot long wooden rip fence that I could clamp to the table and I used this makeshift table saw to make two custom desks for our home office. A picture of the desk I made for my wife appears below.

Every piece of this desk was cut using the $99.00 table saw on the table I constructed. That included ripping the tops, both drawer cabinets, and all the drawer sides, bottoms, and fronts.

It is a simple design with a clear coated plywood top with double round over edges. The draw fronts were made of the same plywood and allowed to extend ½-inch beyond each side of the cabinet to serve as drawer pulls and eliminate the need for metal hardware.

Once I completed my home shop I gave the $99.00 table saw away. A picture of my home shop under construction is on the next page with more information about table saws.

While it isn't necessary to invest in a commercial-duty table saw, you should make certain that your saw is solid and capable of precision cutting. Your space limitations should definitely influence your choice.

A picture of my home shop appears below. Since it isn't for business purposes and I didn't want it to dominate my back yard, it is only fourteen feet by twenty-two feet. It was designed to serve a dual purpose. It has an eight foot by fourteen foot tool storage section and a fourteen by fourteen combination work area and deck. This is not an ideal situation for a woodworking business but it works great for me.

The photo shows construction materials covered on a set of saw horses and it still had not been painted but you can tell how it was designed. To accommodate this space I bought a table saw that was sturdy and accurate yet portable so I could easily put it in the storage area. Pictures of the table saw I selected appear below.

To be able to rip larger pieces of sheet goods I build a couple of simple, table saw height, run off tables. This table saw in my small home shop is presently serving me well to custom build all the kitchen cabinets in my home. Here are a few pictures of the completed parts of the cabinets that were cut entirely with the pictured table saw and assembled with a pneumatic nailer and screws. The doors were cut from solid poplar and assembled using a biscuit joiner.

Notice the custom features in these cabinets, including the bookcase and the microwave and radio space. Before installing the cabinets we had an electrician add receptacles to accommodate the microwave oven and the radio.

The doors on the upper cabinets have rain glass panels that obscure the contents of the cabinets but still allow you to see inside. Custom touches like this and building the cabinets 31 ¾-inches tall instead of the normal 30 inches are possible when cabinets are custom designed for customers. These minor changes add interior space, take full advantage of the sheet goods size, make the cabinets much more functional for the individual customer, and helps grow your business.

The details and pictures of cabinets are not included to impress you with anything except the idea that it isn't necessary to buy a commercial-duty table saw to be in the woodworking business. It is important to own or buy a good, solid table saw and take the time to read the instructions and properly align and true it to ensure accuracy for all your work. Your customers will not care if your table saw costs $200.00 or $2,000.00 as long as you deliver first class work. That is the important thing.

You can improve the accuracy and ease of use of any table saw with an after-market rip fence. These fences are considerably longer than most standard fences that come with table saws and can be helpful when working with sheet goods such as plywood and medium density fiberboard. Large sheets are difficult to rip to size without a good fence. Some table saws will not accommodate these after market fences and you may need to build attachments to make the existing fence longer and more stable.

You should also build portable tables for each side and at the rear of your table saw to accommodate the width and run off of large sheets as you rip them to size. This will make your work easier and safer. The table saw and the area immediately surrounding it can serve as a major work area after you have cut the materials for your projects.

It is easier and more comfortable to assemble cabinets and furniture on a large work surface. Lowering the blade on your table saw will facilitate this and other activities that require a large flat surface. If the work requires any painting, be sure to cover all the surfaces before you begin to avoid making a mess of them.

Alternative To Ripping Sheet Goods On A Table Saw

I've always enjoyed working alone but as I've gotten older it has become more difficult to handle large, thick, sheet goods while ripping on my table saw. Recently, I decided to take advantage of an idea that I used years ago to cut doors. This involved a saw guide that not only kept the saw cutting straight but protected the surface of the material.

Since I wanted it exclusively for sheet goods it had to be much longer than the one I had for doors. I made two of them for ease of handling. One was an eight-foot unit for ripping sheet goods and the other was a four-foot unit for crosscutting sheet goods. Drawings and photos of these saw guides appear on pages 50 and 51.

To make the best possible use of these saw guides I used some 2X4s to create a good cutting surface that would protect my tables from the saw blade and keep the sheet goods flat while I made my cuts. A drawing and picture of this simple cutting surface also appears on pages 50 and 51. I built mine to fit a certain table but the size can be altered to fit any size table or work bench.

Saw guides are not an original idea and you can buy some excellent units that are quite easy to use. The really expensive ones come with a built-in saw that is held in place throughout the cut. There are also metal rip guides you can use but these guide the saw but do not protect the surface and the base of the saw can scratch fine surfaces. Whatever saw guide you use, remember that it must be clamped down solidly to the material surface before beginning a cut. Failure to do this could cause the guide to slip, ruin a rip, and perhaps cause a dangerous kickback.

The one disadvantage of this kind of guide is that the saw is only guided on one side so it's important to proceed with the cut carefully and use both hands to guide the power saw and keep it tight and flat against the guiding edge. This is easily done by using one hand to hold the handle and start switch and the other hand to apply slight pressure toward the guide.

If you have a good table saw setup these guides may be completely unnecessary. They are only offered as an option for those who find working with sheet goods difficult.

Saw Guide Drawing, Photos, And Details

On the next two pages there are drawings, pictures, and information about the saw guides made to facilitate ripping and crosscutting sheet goods without a table saw.

These valuable guides are especially helpful because you can avoid running large, cumbersome sheet goods through your table saw. They are easy to build and will save your back.

Since proper use of these guides requires that your saw cut through the material it's important to have a nice, flat surface that you don't mind cutting up. The photos and drawings on the next two pages shows a cutting surface that can be placed on any table and then removed and stored.

Constructing it involved two pieces of 2X4 seventy inches long and four pieces of 2X4 thirty-eight and one half inches long. It was then assembled with three-inch deck screws. To add diagonal strength and facilitate clamping to a table, there are two twelve inch long, mitered corner brackets screwed into the frame.

The photo below shows the 2X4 frame clamped to a six-foot long, heavy-duty, folding table. It could just as easily be clamped to any other kind of table. You could even build a table for it.

The close up photo above shows the saw guide clamped to a piece of ¾-inch plywood resting on the cutting table designed to accommodate sheet goods and the saw guide. A standard circular saw is used to make the cut. A set of quick clamps holds the saw guide in place so it can be attached and released promptly. A detailed drawing of the table and saw guide appears below.

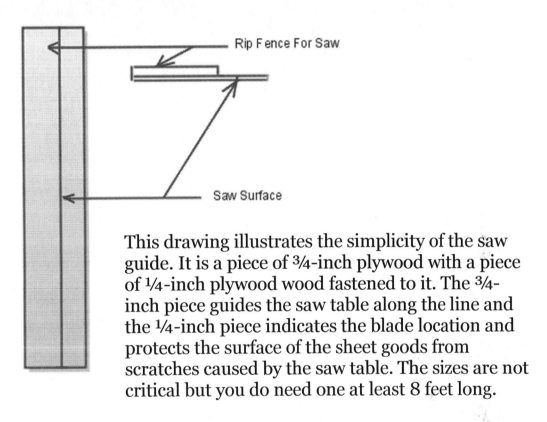

Rip Fence For Saw

Saw Surface

This drawing illustrates the simplicity of the saw guide. It is a piece of ¾-inch plywood with a piece of ¼-inch plywood wood fastened to it. The ¾-inch piece guides the saw table along the line and the ¼-inch piece indicates the blade location and protects the surface of the sheet goods from scratches caused by the saw table. The sizes are not critical but you do need one at least 8 feet long.

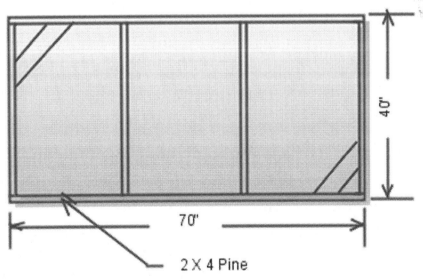

40"

70'

2 X 4 Pine

Crosscutting

In spite of all its flexibility and potential, the table saw is not the best power tool for crosscutting sheet goods unless you own a large, commercial-duty saw with a sliding table. Crosscutting sheet goods on a small, consumer, or even trade-level table saw can lead to dangerous binding and kickbacks that can cause serious injuries.

Obviously, using one of the saw guides previously described is one possibility but you can also build a custom crosscutting jig for your table saw. Pages 53 and 54 include drawings and pictures of a functional and easy to build crosscutting fixture.

The Table Saw Crosscut Fixture

The drawings for building a functional crosscutting fixture for your table saw appears on the next page followed by photos of the crosscut fixture installed on my old Grizzly table saw in my shop many years ago. This particular design would work well on any table saw with grooves for a bevel guide.

These drawings are not to scale and the sizes are certainly not absolute. Making a crosscut fixture involves personal choice based on the kinds of work you will be doing.

You can make your own crosscutting fixture shorter than the seventy inches listed for this one and even make it deeper than the twenty-seven inches listed here. This size will work but you may have a better idea of what will work best for you.

The important thing is to make it sturdy and accurate so that it accurately makes ninety degree cuts through your materials safely to avoid dangerous kickbacks.

Using a crosscut fixture such as this keeps your work pieces in proper alignment ensuring safe crosscutting of all the pieces of any project.

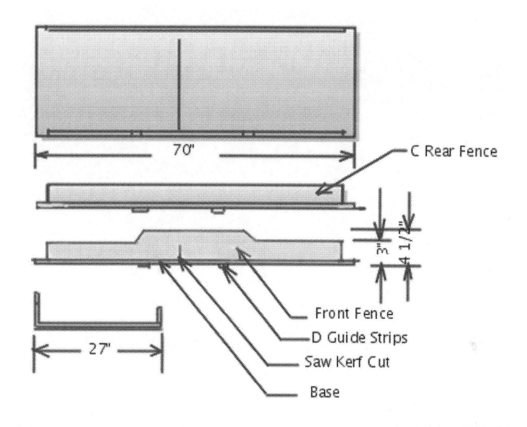

C Rear Fence

4 1/2"

3"

Front Fence

D Guide Strips

Saw Kerf Cut

Base

70"

27"

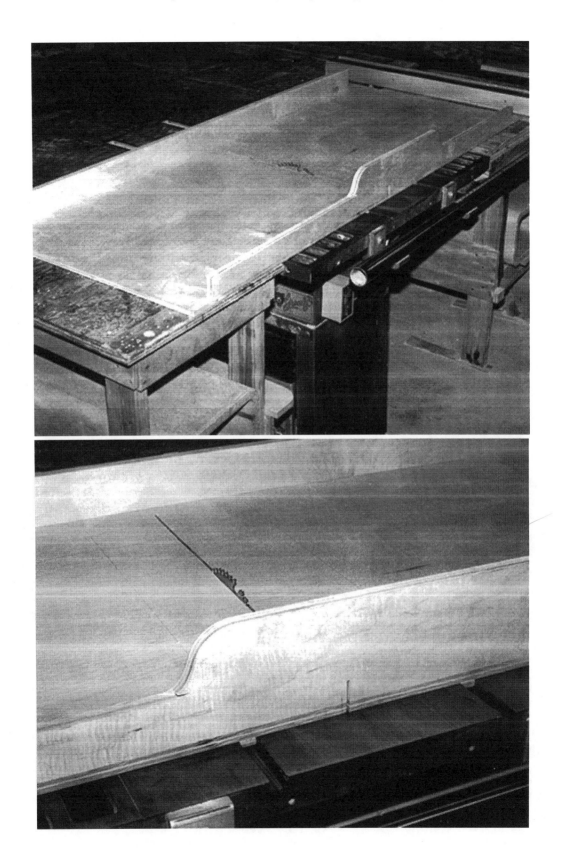

Instructions For The Table Saw Crosscut Fixture

Notice that the front and rear fences must be tall enough to support the base after the blade cuts through. The guide strips must be made to fit your table saw. This size varies among table saws. The corners on these guide strips must be softened slightly with sandpaper and then the strips should be waxed lightly so they slide smoothly and easily.

Also use the sandpaper to soften all the corners on the base of the table saw crosscut fixture so it also slides over the table saw and the side tables easily. The easiest way to accomplish this is to apply a couple of coats of clear wood finish to the base surface to ensure that it slides without resistance.

If you know how to work with plastic laminate, apply a piece of laminate of any color to the bottom of the fixture base. This will help it slide easily. Just be sure to do this before installing the guide strips.

List of Materials

A	1	Base	1/2" X 27" X 70"	Hardwood Plywood
B	1	Front Fence	3/4" X 4 1/2" X 64"	Hardwood Plywood
C	1	Rear Fence	3/4" X 3" X 64"	Hardwood Plywood
D	2	Guide Strips	5/16" X 3/4" X 27"	Solid Hardwood

Remember that these are the dimensions of the crosscut fixture in the photos. You can change these if you prefer your fixture to handle larger pieces or to use it exclusively for smaller pieces.

The guide strips are the correct size for the saw in the photos. It may not work on your saw. Should that be the case, you will have to measure them carefully, make them, and test them in the slots before assembling your crosscut fixture. The fit of the guide strips is important to the accuracy of your crosscuts.

Notice that the photos show a rather simple construction for the crosscut fixture. I view jigs and fixtures as functional shop tools so I don't veneer the edges or do any finishing beyond what is necessary to make sure that the fixture or jig works well. You may feel differently and decide to do a nicely finished project for your fixture. I prefer not to spend the extra time involved in doing this.

The first step is to ensure that the blade of your table saw is in perfect alignment with the bevel guide grooves. This is something you should do even if you don't use a crosscut fixture. The instructions that came with your table saw will assist with these adjustments as necessary.

To begin the assembly of your crosscut jig, lower the blade completely so it clears the top of the table and place the guide strips in the bevel guide grooves. Since these should be a little thinner than the depth of the miter tracks, you will probably have to place a small shim under them. Run a thin strip of glue down the center of the guide strips and then place the base on them gently. The glue helps to keep these strips in the proper position when you are working with the fixture.

Carefully align the base with the top of the table saw to ensure that the blade will also align with the base of the fixture. Either use small, countersunk screws or pneumatic nails to fasten the guide strips to the base. Allow the glue to dry and then remove the base from the table saw and complete the fixture by fastening the front and rear fences.

Now place the crosscut fixture back on the table saw in the rear most position. Start the table saw and slowly crank up the blade to cut completely through the base to the depth necessary to cut though sheet goods. Once the blade has reached the correct height for this clearance, slowly push the crosscut fixture forward until the blade cuts through the rear fence of the fixture.

Your crosscut fixture is now ready. Be sure to keep it out of the weather so it remains completely accurate and easy to use. As a final safety touch you can apply red paint to a small area on each side of the blade path.

The Radial Arm Or Sliding Compound Miter Saw

As effective as a crosscutting jig may be, a good power saw especially designed for crosscutting is a valuable addition to any shop. There was a time when almost every woodworking shop had a radial arm saw. These are useful power tools and still can be used if you already own one. However, you may find that the sliding compound miter saw is a better alternative.

The sliding compound miter saw exhibits a major difference from the radial arm saw that makes it much easier to use for crosscuts that are not at ninety degrees. The important difference when cutting angles with the radial arm and the sliding compound miter saw is described in detail below.

The radial arm saw changes angles by swinging on the large metal support post at the rear of the arm. Because of this, the arm must swing to the right or left to be set for cutting at any angle. This process requires raising the blade to clear the table before changing angles and changes the position of the entire motor and blade from the ninety degree path to the right or left side of ninety degrees. Cutting at several angles is time-consuming and leaves cuts through the rear fence and on the table for every different angle.

On the sliding compound miter saw, the entire table rotates with the motor and the blade to each angle from the exact center of the cutting path. So, regardless of the angle you are cutting, the line of the cut bypasses the rear fence in the same place. Since the entire table rotates, the saw cut is always in exactly the same position relative to the table surface so there is only one cut in the table.

These differences are significant if you have to buy a crosscutting power saw. If you already own a radial arm saw, I would not invest in the sliding compound miter saw until the business can afford the expenditure. The radial arm saw, even with its shortcomings, performs well as a crosscutting tool.

If you do buy a sliding compound miter saw, invest in one with a ten inch or larger blade if possible. This will allow you to crosscut thicker and wider boards easily. Here again, you should buy the best equipment that you can afford.

Final Note On Radial Arm Saws

Radial arm saws have one significant advantage over sliding compound miter saws; they can be used for ripping lumber or sheet goods. By turning the motor and blade completely sideways you can rip large sheets. It is critical to read the safety instructions for this procedure as turning the motor and blade in the wrong direction can toss a piece of material across your shop and seriously injure someone. Handled correctly the radial arm saw can be an effective power tool for ripping sheet goods.

When I first started on a tight budget, my shop was comprised of two twelve foot by twenty four foot storage areas back to back. This gave me a basic tunnel twelve feet wide and forty eight feet long. While not an ideal shop space, the rent was quite low and that helped during startup.

In spite of the strange configuration, it worked well for a couple of years because I used a radial arm saw against one wall for both ripping and crosscutting sheet goods. This is an example of making the best use of what you have available while growing your business.

Five

Hand Tools

Many hand tools are also important for a functional woodworking shop. These can include hammers, mallets, chisels, gouges, screwdrivers, knives, awls, and many others. Again, it is advisable to buy those that you don't already have when you need them for a specific job. This way your collection will grow over time without a large up front investment.

Basic Hand Tools To Get Started

Hammers – you should have several hammers including a claw hammer, a small sledge hammer, a dead-blow hammer, and a ball-peen hammer. A hammer may not be considered a common part of the woodworkers shop but sometimes they are necessary.

The dead blow hammer with the soft rubber surface and the extra impact it transmits can be quite useful during the assembly process. The other hammers can be helpful during some installations.

Screwdrivers – You never know what kind or size of screwdriver may be needed for a job. I suggest purchasing a fairly complete set including flat, phillips, square, and torx in various sizes. A screwdriver is often needed for the assembly of cabinet components.

Chisels – Chisels play an important role in fine woodworking and it's important to have at least a small collection of wood chisels for certain tasks. A set with the sizes ¼ inch, ½ inch, ¾ inch, and 1 inch should be enough to start.

Pry Bars – Also known as Crow Bars, may be handy during installations and they can be useful during those unfortunate times when a mistake is made and a cabinet must be disassembled. A large Crow Bar and a much smaller, flat pry bar are useful.

Nail Set – Three sizes because these can be handy when it's necessary to set new or existing nails. It is possible that you will not be using nails for any of your cabinets but if you are, a nail set will prepare nails for filler before painting or finishing the project.

Awl – Get two of these because they are so easy to lose. Definitely a handy tool for any shop.

Hand Saw – At least one good, sharp hand saw because there are some things for which a power saw is inadequate.

Hack Saw – For those times when cutting metal is necessary and a saber saw is inappropriate. You may run into metal parts that require hand cutting as part of building certain projects.

Coping Saw – For small fine cuts that may be necessary in some repair jobs. The saber saw performs well for many of these functions but sometimes a coping saw is the ideal tool for these cuts.

Mallets – Various mallets are helpful when a hammer might damage surfaces. When using chisels or gouges, a wooden mallet is preferable to either a metal or dead blow hammer. Although the dead blow hammer also does a good job, the wooden mallet has a better and more natural feel to it.

Pliers – Various size and shape pliers including needle nose. These tools can be a lifesaver. You may not need it often but when the need arises, it is an invaluable tool.

Block Plane – These small planes are useful for smoothing out edges and softening corners. The few times you need this tool it will be a lifesaver. You should keep the blade razor sharp.

Jack Plane – For smoothing out larger surfaces such as door edges. The use of this and the block plane will depend on how much solid lumber you are using. These are not useful tools for sheet goods but they are excellent tools for solid wood.

Knives – Several utility knives with extra blades come in handy for cutting many things including for opening boxes.

Wrenches – Several different sizes including crescent and pipe wrenches. These are critical tools if you plan to do your own installation of cabinets.

Levels – Small and large levels. One at least four feet long. Since all cabinets should be installed level, these are critical tools to have when installing cabinets.

Squares – A framing square and an adjustable square. All cabinets and furniture should be perfectly square and a framing square is helpful for this task. However, it is always better to use the diagonal measurement techniques to determine if a project is square.

Tin Snips – At least one pair. Make certain it is a good and sharp one so you can cut various metals, screening, speaker cloth, and other materials easily.

Cold Chisels – Handy for chipping cement when necessary. This is another tool that may not seem necessary for a woodworker but if you will be installing cabinets, some situations may involve chipping cement and, if kept sharp, this tool handles that well.

Tape Measures – One twelve to sixteen feet long and then one at least thirty feet long to measure larger areas. In most cases the small tapes will work but if you plan to do kitchens or other large projects the longer tape will be helpful.

Caulking Gun – A necessary tool to seal spaces between walls and cabinets. It is especially useful when installing laminate counter tops to seal all surfaces against potential water damage.

Staplers - A handy tool for fastening thin materials such as speaker cloth or various kinds of upholstery to cabinets and furniture.

Brushes – For some touch up painting that may be required when cabinets are installed.

Rasps - These come in handy for removing wood rapidly from curved surfaces. Rasps have a flat surface to work on various contours and a round surface to work on concave areas. They leave a rough surface to be smoothed by other tools.

Clamps – Depending on how you will be assembling your cabinets and furniture, a large collection of various size clamps will serve you well. For gluing up boards pipe clamps are an excellent choice but there are many other kinds available now.

Saw Horses – If you don't have sufficient space for permanent work tables, saw horses can be useful to set up work tables when necessary and then disassemble them when the work is completed. Saw horses raise the work surface and make things easier on your back. The folding, plastic units will work but they are somewhat shaky for use as a work table. You will probably be better off either building your own saw horses or purchasing the metal brackets that make it easy to create saw horses using only 2X4 lumber.

Six

Shop Space Or On Site

The ideal way to build cabinet and furniture projects is in your own shop space. This is not only best for you but also for your customers who won't have to put up with all the sawdust and odor involved when building cabinets and furniture. Nevertheless, there are cabinetmakers who work on site. That is, they either build the cabinets in their final location or use the customer's garage or other storage area to assemble the project.

Building cabinets in their final location is not ideal and it is very disruptive to your customers. Cabinets should be completely assembled before being installed on the job site and should not be permanently fastened to the walls of a home or office. They should be attached after completion using screws so it is possible to remove them if necessary.

Working on site, even in a customer's garage space is definitely not ideal and most often creates considerable discomfort for customers. You could lose many potential customers if you work in this fashion. Such an arrangement may end well but could just as easily turn into an unpleasant situation. Even if agreed upon before the job begins, the customer's discomfort may cost you recommendations to friends and family. On the other hand, if your cabinet work is part of a large remodeling job by some contractor, this level of disruption may not be a problem because it is common during the remodeling of a home or office.

Start With Your Own Garage or Storage Space

If you already have a garage or storage space that you can use as a shop, then you are well ahead of others who must find a space to rent. Make certain you find out if local laws allow you to have a commercial shop on your property. In addition to local regulations you must consider any deed restrictions in your subdivision. In some areas even a small shop for personal use is discouraged because of the potential for noise. If you live in a rural area there will probably be few such issues.

Having your own garage or storage space will also save you money in rent. If you do have to rent a space, cost should be a major consideration. Location is important but there is no need to spend for a high cost location that would normally be used for a retail store. What you need is a place where the noise of your machines will not be a problem. A store front is not normally necessary since most of your selling will be done by advertising and by visiting the home or businesses of your customers.

With a shop space, the bigger the better. Nevertheless, there is no need to invest a large amount in rent when first getting started. A shop space of approximately twenty feet by twenty-four feet or larger is a good size to get started. Depending on the size projects that you will be building, this size will serve you for a long time.

Organize Your Shop

Organizing your shop space for efficiency is important but how it is finally set up will depend on the size and final shape of the space. With a large space and two fair size entrances you can set things up so that materials come in and are stored near one entrance and completed projects are loaded for delivery and installation from the second entrance.

My first space was in a storage facility that had back to back spaces. In time I moved to one of the spaces that had the dividing wall removed giving me a twelve foot by forty-eight foot shop. It seemed to be a long tunnel but it allowed me to set up so that materials came in one of the large overhead doors and completed cabinets were loaded into my truck through the overhead door on the other side. That space served me well for several years.

That space was five hundred and seventy-six square feet. As my business grew I moved into larger quarters. My next shop was over seven hundred square feet in a small industrial area and from there I moved to a nearby eleven hundred square foot shop. My last shop was a metal building of fourteen hundred square feet that served me until I retired from woodworking. A picture of that shop appears below.

This shop had a large, twenty foot wide, door for bringing in materials and taking out completed projects and a porch-like cover over the door making it easy to load cabinets into my truck or trailer even when it was raining.

With a smaller space and only one major entrance it may be necessary to set up the space so that materials come in and completed projects go out of the same entrance, as I did with my last shop. This doesn't mean that the space can't be planned efficiently. It simply means that you will have to plan more carefully because of the lack of a second overhead door. You should still set aside a space for material storage, especially for sheet goods. In a small space you will need to create this storage area so the sheet goods are stored standing on end. This facilitates much more material in a smaller floor space.

For lumber, you can create simple racks on the wall so it doesn't take up much-needed floor space. Careful planning is important and you may have to make changes several times after completing projects until you arrive at the design that is most workable for the kind of work that you do most.

Basically, you can create sections for material storage, cutting, assembly, finishing, and final assembly. The final assembly section is critically important if you are building cabinets or furniture in modules because you will want to assemble the unit completely to see exactly how everything fits together before final installation. It's embarrassing to deliver a piece that does not come together as planned. Even when everything is planned, problems can arise.

Does Everything Fit Through The Door?

I once built an entire house full of cabinets for a local attorney. It was a large job that included all the kitchen cabinets, cabinets in three bathrooms, and some special cabinets in the bedrooms and the living room. Everything fit perfectly until I reached the final small bathroom. It was divided into two sections. One section contained a long vanity which went in without difficulty. The other section was entered through a small pocket door. On one side was the water closet and directly across from it was a tall cabinet for storing towels and other bathroom supplies and the bottom section was a built-in clothes hamper. The cabinet looked great but because of the small size of the room, the low ceiling, and the narrow door, the cabinet could not be put into the room. I had to take it back to my shop and redesign it in two pieces and then bring it back to install. Since everything else went so perfectly the customer just had a laugh about it but I found it embarrassing. The lesson is, make certain that cabinets will fit through the doors.

As your business grows and a larger space becomes necessary, keep your costs in mind. Don't commit to rents that are difficult to pay if work gets slow. Keep your costs for shop space as low as possible as this will increase your profit. Don't be concerned that your customers might consider your shop too small to do their work. Most customers have no idea what size shop it takes to do various jobs. In any case, they are almost always concerned with the quality of your work, not the size of your shop.

A Showroom?

During all the years that I operated my woodworking business, I never had a showroom for my customers to visit. A showroom is not necessary for the one-person woodworking business. Customers who visit showrooms are unlikely to call you. And, if they do it will be because they are looking for lower prices than those at the large companies with showrooms.

Have a good photo collection of your work in an album and on a web site so prospects can see the kind of work you are capable of doing. As soon as possible, collect some testimonials from customers who are willing to tell people about the quality of your work and your professionalism. Word of mouth is an excellent way to get more work.

Seven

Licensing, Accounting, And Taxes

The requirements for businesses, whether home-based or regular commercial establishments, will vary from one community to another. It's critical that you learn exactly what is required in your community before opening for business. The differences among communities may surprise you if you move from one city to another and could create problems for you.

I lived in Tampa, Florida for many years where I was required to buy an occupational license to run my woodworking shop. However, when I moved to Austin, Texas there was no such requirement. As required in Florida, I did have to get a sales tax certificate so I could collect and pay the sales tax. So, one community had a different requirement for licensing while both states required a certificate for collecting sales tax.

I also found out that both states collected a Tangible tax which is basically an annual tax on the value of the equipment that you use in your business. Not only do you pay for your equipment and pay sales tax when purchasing it, but you also have to pay an annual tax on the value of any equipment that you use in your business.

Take the time to research any licensing or taxes that your community or state charges businesses operating within their boundaries. This will save you time and possibly fines for failure to adhere to local laws.

The Internal Revenue Service

Most of you have probably been paying income taxes to the IRS for years. If you have worked for an employer of reasonable size, your income tax preparations are fairly simple. Your employer deducts the taxes from your income and gives you a form annually describing exactly how much you made during the year and how much was deducted for income taxes and Social Security. This makes the preparation of your annual income tax forms fairly simple and inexpensive even if filed by an income tax preparation company.

Keep Track of All Possible Deductions

That will change when you begin your own business because, in addition to your income, you must also keep track of all your costs so you can deduct them from your income. Failure to keep good records of income and expenses could create serious problems with the IRS. For this reason I strongly recommend that you buy an accounting software program and take the time to learn how to use it effectively. And, follow through by keeping up with your accounting regularly.

If you are fortunate enough to have someone such as a family member or close friend who can handle these tasks for you at a reasonable cost, by all means take advantage of that. Just make absolutely certain that the records are being kept accurately and you receive regular, at least monthly, reports on the status of your accounts.

Using Checking Account Statements For Accounting

If you only plan to run your woodworking business on a part-time basis, you can save time and money by using your checking account statements for required record keeping. To do this, you must open a checking account that is used solely for your woodworking business activities. This is something you should do anyway. It is unwise to mix business costs with your personal funds because that is certain to cause confusion and accounting difficulties.

Once you have your checking account open, make certain that all the income from your woodworking business is deposited into that checking account. Pay all the bills of the woodworking business from that checking account by using checks or a debit card. Handled in this way, it is easy to use the monthly statements for record keeping. Each month, when you receive your statement and reconcile it, simply identify the purpose of every expense for income tax purposes.

For simplicity, you could create a numbering system that assigns each kind of expense a number. Then you simply have to place the correct number next to the expense and put the statements in a folder for use at the end of the year to calculate your taxes.

Keep Clear and Concise Records

No matter what method you use to keep your accounting up to date, make certain that you keep good records and receipts for all of your expenses. Your business related expenses and the cost of any tools you buy are deductible from the money you make but only if you keep good records.

You can deduct any rent, electricity, water, gas, phone, Internet connections, and any other expenses that are directly related to your business activities. You can also depreciate any equipment you buy and in many cases you can deduct the full amount of the purchase during the same year that you bought it. You should make certain that you check this out with the IRS or with an accountant before completing your income tax forms for each year.

Accounting software includes invoicing but if you are using bank statements for accounting, you will need invoices for some of your customers. It's a simple task to find a small and free invoice creation program on the Internet. Just do a search on Google or Yahoo and you will find several. To cross-reference specific invoices with deposits on your bank statement you can simply put the invoice numbers next to the deposits. Remember, this is only workable for limited earning, part-time businesses.

Save For Your Income Taxes

You should either arrange to pay estimated income tax on your woodworking income every quarter or open a savings account in which to deposit a percentage of every job for paying your taxes. If your business income becomes fairly high, the IRS will send you forms to accommodate your payment of estimated taxes. Failure to pay these taxes will almost certainly accrue a penalty and interest. Estimated tax is a good idea because it avoids a large tax bill at the end of the year. It is basically a payroll deduction method for small businesses.

Pay Your Taxes On Time

No matter how you decide to handle your income tax obligations, make certain that you handle them by the prescribed due dates. If for some reason you are unable to pay your taxes in full, file your income tax form on time and send in a check for as much as you can afford. You will receive a bill for the balance with penalty and interest added.

If you still can't pay, contact the IRS and make arrangements to pay them in installments. Do not ignore them or fail to file an annual income tax form. Sooner or later they will come to get their money and the penalties and interest will be a serious amount.

Eight

Getting Started

There are definite steps to take when getting started. After you have all the licensing and tax issues worked out and have organized your shop in preparation for woodworking jobs, it's time to get people interested in your woodworking business so you can convert them into paying customers.

Look Professional

The first critical step in finding customers is to look like a real business. You may be a one-person business but that is no reason to look unprofessional. Create or purchase business cards and some nice stationery. These need not be expensive but they shouldn't look cheap either. There are several ways to create business cards for yourself. You can print them in small quantities by purchasing the necessary business card paper at an office supply place and then use a simple business card software to create them.

Simpler yet, you can contact the VistaPrint company and they will make all your business cards, stationary, postcards, small signs, etc. at good prices. They even have quite a few products that are free except for shipping costs. As long as you don't try to have them shipped quickly those costs are reasonable. They have excellent templates so you can quickly create a good business card or other related stationery. You can get to their web site at: http://vistaprint.com.

You also need to have all the necessary contract documents printed and ready for your first customer. It is unprofessional to scribble out agreements on the spot when you are dealing with a job for which you expect payment. Contracts should be neat and serious documents that make it clear that you will do the described work but also expect prompt and full payment for your efforts. A contract and related forms appears in chapter ten.

Photo Album and Web Site

Create a photo album with pictures of all the projects you have built for yourself, family members, or friends. This album shows your prospects the quality of work that you are capable of doing for them. The photographs used for this album can serve a dual purpose if you use them to create a web site that will be available twenty-four hours a day to all interested prospects. For information on how to create your own small business web site using free software and hosting it at the lowest available cost contact me at: bill@positive-imaging.com .

Contact Everyone!

Now that you have everything in place for contacting everyone you know, start with your family and friends. Contact them by phone, email, mail, text message, whatever method you believe is best for the person you are contacting. It may be best to contact some people with more than one method. You may get the best results from some people by contacting them in person. Tell them exactly what you are doing and ask them to tell everyone they know about your new business. Give them extra business cards and make certain it lists your web site.

You might also consider telling everyone that you are starting out with bargain pricing to generate interest and introduce yourself to more customers who can then refer you to others. This may work especially well because word of mouth advertising is always the best way to find customers.

Advertise Carefully To Avoid Waste

Advertise your business carefully. It is easy to over spend on advertising and get little, if any, benefit. Try to identify your best prospects and how to reach them. A good place to start is with local weekly newspapers. The ads cost much less than the daily papers and they are kept around for a whole week instead of just a day.

Don't hesitate to use your vehicle for advertising your services. I had a hand-made wooden sign on the tailgate of my pickup truck and it often got me jobs.

On more than one occasion someone followed me for a while and then approached me about a job once I stopped. A picture of that wooden sign appears below.

Use The Internet

Don't overlook the Internet for advertising. Get your web site noticed by mentioning it in every ad. Place it as a signature on every email, blog, facebook, twitter, or any other Internet connection you make. Let people see the link so they will visit the site and see what you can do for them. Your web site address is one long word that can put prospects in touch with your photo album and information about your business.

Remember that the emphasis of any advertising you do for your woodworking business should be on the prospect, not on you. Potential customers want to know what is in it for them. Tell them why it is in their best interest to deal with you.

Give Everyone A Business Card

Remember to have your business cards with you at all times because you never know when you will be sharing information about your business with someone. Even though this has been covered before, it bears repeating. With your business card you should have some brief information about the work you do so you can share it with anyone in just a few seconds. Be ready when you get the chance to make an impression. You never know when someone will be interested in the kind of work you do.

Keeping Customers

Getting customers is critical but keeping customers after you acquire them is even more important. It can cost eight to ten times as much to get a new customer as to hold on to one you already have. How do you go about making certain that you keep every customer for whom you do a job?

Step one is to always let your customers know that you value their business. Treat them as if they were the most important part of your business because they are. Without them, there is no business. This has two-fold benefits because in addition to the continued business from the customer, he or she will recommend your products and services to others.

Step two is handling mistakes promptly and properly. While it is certainly important to establish and maintain a firm reputation for quality work and reliability, you will make mistakes. The customer service you provide when these mistakes occur will determine whether you keep or lose a customer.

Admit Your Mistakes

Many people seem to find it difficult to admit mistakes but this is where you must start and follow up immediately taking steps to correct the mistakes without being pressured by the customer. With the present lack of good customer service in many industries, you have a unique opportunity to impress your customers and keep them coming back.

If you believe, as some people do, that being right is the most important thing, your business is certain to suffer financially. When things go wrong in any business transaction, the most important thing is how your customer feels when the incident is over. That will determine whether they return and if they will recommend you to others.

Good customer service is the key. It is more important now than ever because it is becoming very difficult to get good service. Think about the last time you got really good customer service at any business. It was memorable because of the poor service you normally get. That level of service is what you must give your customers every day. Make it impossible to forget the great experience of doing business with you.

Here are a couple of examples from my personal experience. One is about how to lose a good customer and the other is how to keep a customer even when a problem arises. The first happened to a competitor of mine. He had contracted to build a custom desk for a customer. He completed the desk and the customer told him that the desk should have had a lock on one of the drawers. My competitor insisted that it was not part of the price. He finally installed the lock and billed the customer for an extra $16.00. The customer paid it but was disturbed by being billed. My competitor refused to give the customer any satisfaction on the issue.

About a month later I received a call from this same company to quote them for some office furniture. They were opening a second office and wanted several pieces of custom furniture including custom desks and a file cabinet. I submitted a quote and got the job. I later found out that my price was higher than my competitor's price for the same pieces but I got the job because the manager was still upset about the $16.00. So, for this small amount my competitor gave up a contract of several thousand dollars. Of course, I was glad that he had to be right since it got me a very good contract. More importantly, it got me a good customer who ordered products from me many more times after that first experience.

On another job, I built a conference table for a law office and they didn't like the appearance of the top. I told the customer to use the existing top for a couple of weeks and I would build a new one for them just the way they wanted it. Two weeks later I arrived with a new top and switched it out. They were well satisfied with the new top and gave me a contract to install crown molding throughout their entire office. The original top was acceptable but it just wasn't the way they pictured it and it was obvious that I didn't understand exactly what they wanted. In addition to the new work, I got recommended to other law offices. As to the top that I took back, it served me for many years as an assembly table. I just placed it on a couple of specially built, low profile, saw horses in my shop.

Good customer service pays off and it's the right thing to do. I suggest that you put yourself in your customer's shoes before making a decision on any customer service issue. Determine how you would like to be treated if you were facing the same situation and treat your customer at least as well.

Nine

Setting Prices

Setting prices for your work is always difficult because of so many potential variables. Nevertheless, you have to set prices and those prices must be accurate in two ways. First, your prices must be low enough to make sure that you are competitive so you can stay in business. Secondly, your prices must be high enough to allow a reasonable profit to make your business activities financially worthwhile.

There are concise methods for calculating the price of any project regardless of the complexity. Obviously, you will face variables depending on the kind of project and the specific customer. These must be taken into account to ensure accuracy.

How Much Do You Want To Make?

To a one-person business, this is an especially important question. Ask yourself specifically how much you want to get paid for each hour you spend working on your business. This is the first decision when setting prices.

You also need to decide how much profit you want to make from your woodworking business. You can't set a price for any job until you know how much you want to make. Now is the time to make those decisions. Come up with a firm hourly figure and a firm percentage of profit you would like to make from every job you take on. These figures are essential to your pricing calculations.

Take your time establishing an hourly figure for your work because this is the hourly figure that you will apply to every project or product. Remember that this is only what you want to be paid for your time and should not include the cost of materials or any other costs related to specific jobs. Those calculations will come later.

The Hourly Figure

In establishing this hourly figure, try to balance reality with desire. Obviously, you want to get paid as much as possible for your time but you must balance this amount with what is possible in your market. Let's assume you want a minimum of $25 per hour for your time. We will use that figure for our calculations but you must decide what this figure will be in your own job cost calculations. It can be more or less depending on what you feel is right for your area. There is no wrong answer. Find out what other woodworkers are charging. You are not stuck with their figures but it helps to have a realistic idea when you are getting started.

Your Shop Space Costs

The next step is the cost for shop space. Even if you use your own garage or utility building, you must consider the cost of shop space. Don't think that just because you have a space that there is no direct cost. This could be a serious mistake since your garage and driveway will become busy and neighbors may complain. You could be forced to move into a commercial location to satisfy your neighbors and keep peace in the neighborhood.

If you are renting a shop space, you can use the actual cost. Otherwise, determine this cost by checking out commercial spaces of similar size. Use this figure to calculate the monthly rent and add for utilities such as electricity, water and telephone. Even if you don't have separate utilities for your business, use a portion of the home utilities cost to determine an accurate amount. For example, you could take twenty percent of your mortgage payment, electric and telephone bill of $1,000.00. This total would be $200.00 per month.

Once you know the monthly amount it has to be converted to an hourly amount. To determine this amount you need to decide how many hours a month you will be working. For the sake of simplicity, assume you will be working 160 hours per month. Divide the $200.00 rent figure by 160 for a total of $1.25 per hour.

Buying and Maintaining Your Tools

You either already have or will be acquiring a fair collection of woodworking tools. Some of these will be large stationary power tools including table saws, radial arm saws, sliding compound miter saws, band saws, thickness planers, etc. Others are portable power tools that include circular saws, reciprocal saws, saber saws, sanders, and biscuit jointers. Still others are hand tools such as hammers, mallets, chisels, rasps, hand saws, knives, planes, etc. These tools not only involve an initial investment but they must be maintained in good working order. Over the years they will need to be replaced with newer or better models.

All of these costs have to be considered. Over time, when tools need to be replaced, you will need the funds to pay for such replacement. The process of equipment getting old and requiring replacement is called depreciation. You must set up a depreciation schedule and deposit funds into a bank account to pay for the equipment when it requires replacement. Failure to do this will mean that you have to pay for these tools from funds intended for other purposes.

In addition to replacement, you depreciate tools for income tax purposes. Even after a tool has been depreciated completely for income tax purposes, the depreciation schedule should continue to ensure that funds are available for the replacement of tools. For example, a good table saw may serve you for twenty years with proper maintenance and sharp blades. Nevertheless, you will probably be able to depreciate a table saw completely for income tax purposes after five years. Then you can continue to set aside funds and use the equipment for as long as possible. This will help your savings to grow and you will always be prepared to replace any equipment as necessary.

The easiest way to do this is to establish an annual depreciation figure based on the total cost of your tools and the years you expect them to last. Let's assume that the value of your tools works out to about $2,800.00 per year for five years. To calculate this you would divide $2,800.00 by 12 for a total of $233.00 a month for the replacement and maintenance of tools. Then divide the $233.00 by the 160-hour figure we established earlier, this would require $1.45 per hour.

A Work Vehicle

To carry materials and deliver projects you need a work vehicle and the maintenance and fuel required to run that vehicle. The actual cost of the vehicle is covered as depreciation as with your equipment. Let's assume that your vehicle cost $18,000.00 and you expect it to last for five years. At the end of five years the depreciated value of your vehicle will be about $3,000.00. That means the amount you can deduct for depreciation is $15,000.00. Simply divide the $15,000.00 by 60 months and then divide that sum by 160 hours. This gives you a total of $1.56 per hour.

From the standpoint of depreciation for income tax purposes you may be able to deduct the entire amount of the vehicle depreciation during the first year. You should check this out with IRS depreciation rules. This in no way changes the need for depositing these funds for future replacement. Remember, a deduction reduces your taxes but you still have to put funds aside if you want to replace the vehicle at some time. It may be several years before your vehicle requires replacement and when that day comes you will be ready if you have deposited the funds.

Maintaining and Fueling Your Vehicle

Determining your maintenance and fuel cost requires keeping good records. Let's assume that it will cost $300.00 per month to keep your vehicle properly maintained and fueled. This would require $1.88 per hour. Remember that these figures are only for your purposes. You will have to keep concise records of either your auto expenditures or your exact mileage used for business to satisfy the requirements of the IRS.

The High Cost of Insurance

Insurance is another high cost item that must be considered. Your vehicle requires adequate insurance to protect you if anything happens to it, you get hurt, or hurt someone else in an accident. But this is only part of the insurance picture. You also need fire, theft, and liability insurance for your business, your shop, job sites, and completed projects.

Unless your spouse has health insurance coverage to which you can be added, you also need health insurance and this can be quite costly. This one expense alone creates many headaches for small businesses. I strongly recommend that you keep at least major medical insurance coverage. It is unlikely that you will be able to get all this insurance coverage for less than $450 per month requiring $2.80 per hour cost.

Remember All Your Taxes

For many, federal income taxes are a nemesis. In truth, taxes are a reality you must face to do business. Unfortunately, it's not uncommon for small businesses to have problems with the IRS, whose job it is to collect federal income taxes. Most of the time, the problems arise as a direct result of failing to make adequate provisions by setting aside funds for the payment of income taxes.

Problems with the IRS can be serious and costly because failure to pay on time will certainly accrue interest and penalties that can quickly double, and even triple your tax obligation. If at all possible, pay your taxes quarterly as required by the IRS. If not, at least open a savings account to save a portion of your income to pay your taxes.

This amount should be at least ten percent of your gross income. Remember, this is ten percent of all the income that comes in, not just what your may pay yourself. This will be a significant amount but that is what you need to be certain you can pay your income taxes on time. It is difficult to estimate the exact amount of your income taxes but you will probably pay from twenty to thirty percent of your net income. Social Security alone is fifteen percent. Remember, unlike employees who pay only one half of the Social Security, while their employer pays the other half, as a small business you must pay the entire amount.

A net income of $30,000.00 per year could cost you approximately $8,000.00 and this would require at least $4.20 per hour. This figure can vary considerably depending on your allowable deductions but it is better to save too much than not enough. Don't forget your state income taxes if applicable in your state. The best plan is to save more than you need. After all, it is going into your savings so whatever is left over can be used for a vacation or anything else you choose.

Pay Yourself For All Your Work

As a one-person woodworking business you will be estimating every job, preparing drawings and bid presentations, picking up materials, running various errands, doing all the required accounting, and many other related items that consume a lot of time. It is important to get paid for that time. It is difficult to charge customers directly for time spent on jobs before you actually get them. Therefore, you have to consider this time as part of your hourly calculations. To get paid for this time you should add at least $400 per month for an hourly amount of $2.50.

Don't Forget The Profit

Even though you love woodworking, your motivation for doing it as a business is probably profit, which is critical to the success of any business. It is important to calculate a fair profit for every job you contract.

There are two ways to calculate your profit on jobs. The first is to make the profit part of the hourly figure. The other is to calculate it separately based on the entire job. A higher percentage must be used if it is part of the hourly figure since the profit calculation does not include materials and you should make a profit on the materials. I suggest that you add the profit, based on at least twenty percent, to the total job. However, if you decide to add it to the hourly figure, use at least twenty-five percent.

You now have a basic list of all the figures necessary to calculate the price on any job. Remember that these are sample figures. You can see how they work here but you must calculate the actual figures for your jobs to determine the pricing for the labor on each job.

Check out the chart on the next page for a breakdown of hourly charges. Start with the figures listed there to calculate your hourly charge. List all the items discussed before and remember that the costs in your area may differ and you may have other priorities to consider. This chart is just an example to help you create your own chart.

How Much To Charge Chart

Hourly Wage (How much you want to make?)	$25.00
Shop Cost ($200 divided by 160 hours)	$01.25
Tool Maintenance ($233 divided by 160 hours)	$01.45
Vehicle ($15,000 cost/60 months divided by 160 hours)	$01.56
Vehicle Maintenance and Fuel ($300 divided by 160 hours)	$01.88
Insurance ($450 divided by 160 hours)	$02.80
Taxes ($8,000/12 months divided by 160 hours)	$04.20
Misc. Overhead ($400 divided by 160 hours)	$02.50
TOTAL PER HOUR	**$40.64**
Profit On Hourly Basis ((25% of Total Hourly Figure Above)	$10.16
TOTAL CHARGE PER HOUR INCLUDING PROFIT	**$50.80**

A Sample Job

For the purposes of a sample job, let's assume that it will take twenty-eight hours to complete the entire job. Just multiply twenty-eight times **$50.80** for a total of **$1,422.00.** This is your total labor and profit on this job. All the figures listed for these samples are rounded up to the nearest dollar.

Cost Of Materials

The next step is to calculate the cost of the materials. Start by using your drawings and related information about the project to prepare a precise materials list. This list should include the quantity of each item. Strive for accuracy here because any mistakes will come right out of your pocket.

Assign an accurate price to each item and, if in doubt, price the item higher rather than lower. You may need to contact some of your suppliers to get updated prices. This should be done regularly as prices do change over time.

There is Always Some Waste

Remember to add a waste factor. Most hardwoods come in random sizes and sheet goods seldom work out evenly so, you will have waste. For this project we will assume the materials will cost **$600.00.** Add the labor and profit amount to the **$600.00** for materials for a total of **$2,022.00**, which is the total price of the job.

If you prefer to add the profit separately, use the **$40.64** figure times twenty eight and that equals **$1,138.00**. Then add the **$600.00** for materials for a total of **$1,738.00**. Calculate twenty percent of **$1,738.00** and it equals **$348.00**. Add **$348.00** to **$1,738.00** to total **$2,086.00**. Notice that the figures from both methods are close.

Since accuracy in setting prices is so important, there is a way you can do one last calculation to check the accuracy of your estimate. Exactly how this calculation is handled depends upon the complexity level of the job.

A Final Check of Your Pricing

When you consider a job to be of average difficulty, simply multiply the cost of materials times **3.5** to get a fairly close estimate. In this case, you would multiply **$600.00** by **3.5** to get a total of **$2,100.00,** which clearly indicates that your calculations for this job are right on target.

For much more complex jobs that take more time, the calculating multiplier should be increased. For example, if you considered this job quite complex and time-consuming and used a multiplier of **4.5,** the total would then be **$2,700.00** and it would be evident immediately that your calculations for the job were inadequate and should be reconsidered. These extra steps will prevent a mistake that could cause your real hourly rate for a job to be reduced.

Check Prices In Your Own Area

Please remember that these figures are not necessarily correct for your area. You will have to do research in your area to determine the prices of all items for your jobs. It is also important to check out what is considered a fair wage for the kind of work you will be doing. The cost of living in your community may be much higher and the income for professionals will also be much higher. Take the time to research this so you don't short change yourself or over charge and lose jobs.

The Rule of Supply and Demand

The rule of supply and demand is one of the most basic rules of business. Unfortunately, it is often overlooked by owners of small businesses. Your prices should always reflect the demand for your work. This is common practice in many businesses.

Check hotel rates during peak and slow seasons to see how they vary. You can also check airfares during various times of the year. When there is low demand, the prices go down to encourage more people to buy. When the demand is high, the prices go up to increase profits and adjust the demand to the available supply.

You can take advantage of the rule of supply and demand as a one-person business. When you have a backlog of work and continue getting more work than you can possibly do in a reasonable amount of time, increase your prices until the work levels off to a flow rate that you can handle. The formula in the previous pages indicates how much you must charge for a job to make a living. It does not indicate how much you can charge for a job if it is sold to someone who knows your work and is willing to pay you more.

The actual amount that you can charge for a job is determined by the customer's willingness to pay, not by any formula. The purpose of the formula is to make certain that you charge enough, avoid losing money, and always make at least a small profit. The right price for anything is the amount a willing buyer will pay a willing seller. Beyond that, there are no limits.

It often seems that there is a preconceived notion that a woodworker running his own one-person business can only make wages and must be ready to sacrifice a decent income, medical benefits, and vacations to do the work he or she loves. Do you really believe that? If you do, it may well be true for you. It is certainly true for many woodworkers. If you know any individual woodworkers who are trying to make a living with the work they love, this may be the case for them. It doesn't have to be that way for you. If you have the skills to produce a good product and charge enough for it, you can make a good living operating your own woodworking business.

FINAL NOTES ON PERCEIVED VALUE AND SUPPLY AND DEMAND

After many years in the woodworking business I learned never to limit myself by what the competition charged. As my backlog increased, I began to raise my prices and found that even people who did not know me personally were willing to pay me more for jobs because of the reputation I had developed. You may also be worth much more to your customers.

Some people are making $10.00 per hour while others make over $100.00 per hour. There may be a significant difference in skills but what often makes the difference is the value the customer perceives. A clear example of this is the art world. One canvas may look beautiful and not be worth the value of *the canvas materials to buyers. Another canvas of the same size may look worthless to you or me yet bring thousands, even millions from art lovers. This is all value perceived by the customer who is willing and able to pay the price.*

Why shouldn't the same thing apply to woodworkers? There are woodworkers who struggle to get a few hundred dollars for a really nice rocking chair and others who are getting thousands for a similar chair. And, the one that is getting thousands has a long waiting list. Perhaps one of those woodworkers is much more skilled and creative than the other but they could be at similar levels. Perceived value is the key ingredient. One of the woodworkers has become famous, perhaps because of books he has written or some other public exposure. Whatever the reason, his work is perceived to have more value. Use perceived value to your advantage. If people really love your work, then charge as much as the market will bear.

If you want to be in business in a free enterprise system, such as ours, you must remember that the price of everything is based on supply and demand. The maximum price of any product or service is the maximum amount that customers are willing to pay for it. If you have a problem with the idea of perceived value and supply and demand and believe that it is somehow unfair to charge more based simply on demand, remember that this could limit your profit significantly and keep you from making a good living.

While it is true that most of you are in woodworking because of love for the work, why shouldn't you make a good living doing the work you love? Doing that over the long-term requires that you charge as much as possible for every job. For maximum profit on every job you must consider perceived value and the rule of supply and demand.

Ten

Contracting Jobs

Contract Forms

Keep your contract forms simple because customers are hesitant to sign long and complex contract forms written in difficult to understand legalese. On the other hand, a contract should protect you in the event that a problem arises during the job.

Remember that a good contract is an agreement between two honest people who want to do some form of business. If one or the other intends to cheat on the arrangement, the contract will not prevent problems. It may protect you but it won't stop problems from arising if you do not perform as agreed or if there is a misunderstanding.

This means that even with a good contract, being right is not the important thing. The best thing is to complete every job with a happy and satisfied customer who will call you again and recommend you to his or her friends and family.

The Steps Of Contracting For Work

Contracting for work involves several steps. The first one is selling the customer on the idea that you are the best person to do the work. This requires finding out exactly what the customer wants. That can only be determined by listening to the customer and making certain you understand what he or she is explaining to you.

Once the job is clear to you, it's wise to prepare some simple drawings and specifications to make sure that you and the customer are on the same page regarding the work to be done. The next step is to calculate the cost of the job and give the customer an accurate and competitive quote.

After all this is complete, if the customer decides to give you the job, the contract form is prepared. The contract should define the job clearly and refer to any drawings or specifications prepared specifically for the job. All of the drawings and any additional specifications should be attached to the contract form. At this point you sign the contract and give it to the customer to sign. Each of you should keep a signed copy of the contract and all related documents.

The Deposit

The next step is one of the most important and often overlooked part of the contracting process. You should always require a fifty percent deposit payable upon execution of the contract, that is, when the contract is accepted and signed by the customer. This amount must be paid before the job starts.

Some will tell you that it is difficult if not impossible to get a fifty percent deposit from customers. That isn't true and you will get little resistance from customers who trust you enough to spend the money for the job. If you have developed a rapport with the customer he or she will not doubt your honesty. If your honesty is in question to any customer, you are better off without the job because such distrust will lead to difficulties almost immediately.

Even when you are first starting your business, it is no problem to get a deposit as long as you present yourself professionally, carefully explain the work, present clear and concise drawings and a fair contract form. When people realize you are serious and know what you are doing, they will not resist the deposit. Once you develop a reputation it will be even easier to get the deposits from your customers.

As previously mentioned, a contract with a customer is based on trust. If a customer is unwilling to sign a contract and give you a deposit, then trust doesn't exist. For whatever reason, the customer is concerned that you will not follow through and perform as you promised. If you relent and proceed without the deposit, you can't be certain that you will get paid.

The fifty percent deposit is a compromise. The customer has a reasonable assurance that you will do your job to get the rest of the money. You have a reasonable assurance you will get paid because the owner has contracted with you and given you a good faith deposit that he or she will not want to lose. If even this limited amount of trust doesn't exist, you should not be doing business with each other.

> *In all my years in the woodworking business what worked for me was to get a fifty percent deposit when the contract was executed (when the customer signed the contract agreeing to the work and the terms). The balance of the contract amount was then payable in full upon satisfactory completion of the work described in the contract. I recommend that you use this procedure to avoid losing money on jobs.*

Forms You Can Use

To help you prepare the forms you need, there is a web site with a sample contract form and many other forms available at:

http://woodworkers-business-guide.com/forms.html

You may use any of these forms and change them with your company name and address. These are forms that worked for years but there is no legal adequacy stated or implied. They are merely supplied to save you time. You may consider getting an attorney to prepare a simple contract for you but do not allow it to become a twenty page nightmare of legal jargon. This will just make it much more difficult to sell your work.

In addition to the forms at the web site listed on the previous page, you can find reduced copies of those forms on pages 101, 102, and 103 and you can use those as a guide to prepare your own forms.

No matter the form of your contract or your reputation, you may rarely run into a potential customer who absolutely refuses to pay the fifty percent deposit. It is important to treat this deposit requirement as standard policy that you do not bypass for anyone. Potential customers who resist the deposit may sometimes come up with various alternatives including various lower percentages or depositing the money for the job in an escrow account.

> *Years ago I had one potential customer who refused to pay the deposit even though she had gotten my name from a neighbor who recommended me highly. Even though it was clear that she wanted me to do the work, she was adamant about not paying the deposit.*

> *The woman continued to call me various times over a couple of months offering alternative proposals and trying to get me to relent on my policy. I finally had to tell her not to call me anymore. I strongly recommend that you set a policy regarding the fifty percent deposit and apply it to everyone. Unless you can afford to lose money on projects, it is the only sensible thing to do.*

Dealing With General Contractors

Remember that this policy will eliminate almost all general contractors as customers. Contractors want to have the work done and then pay you after they get a draw from the bank financing the work. This can be a slippery slope that can cost you a lot of money.

> *I've known several woodworkers over the years who allowed themselves to be talked into doing complete kitchens in large subdivisions thinking they would make a lot of money. As it turned out, some contractors cut their prices after accepting*

their quotes initially. And, several contractors failed to pay at all. They were left with the option of filing liens on the property. They may get paid sooner or later and probably only a portion of what they are owed. Plus, they will have to pay the legal expenses of filing liens on the property.

Some contractors will try to cut your price after the fact because they realize that the home or building is costing more than they estimated. If you stick with your policy, only contractors who have the financial ability to pay the deposit up front will do business with you and your odds of collecting the balance when the job is done are greatly increased.

Sometimes You Don't Need A Contract And Deposit

There are some situations where a contract and deposit arrangement may not be possible or necessary. One of those involves doing work for government agencies. In those cases, it is unlikely that you will not get paid and it may not be possible for them to arrange a deposit or even sign a contract. In most cases governments work with a purchase order arrangement and you will have to accept that if you choose to do work for them.

> *Don't think that you will get paid promptly by government agencies. They will pay you but seldom promptly. Years ago I did a $2,800.00 job for the IRS. I felt since they always have such high expectations for people to pay on time or be charged penalties and interest, they might pay promptly. It didn't turn out that way. It took me more than ninety days after billing them to finally collect my money.*

Another time where deposits could be a problem is with large corporations. They also work with purchase orders so you may have to pass on the deposit if you want their business. You should be very careful here because some corporations are badly managed and some of their employees simply don't care about their vendors and it may take a long time to finally collect.

The last area where a deposit could be overlooked is when doing work for someone regularly. For example, I had a customer who owned rental property on which I did woodworking related repairs for more than ten years. In his case I would just do the jobs and send him a bill and he would send me a check. It would have been too bothersome to do a contract for so many small jobs.

The important thing is to handle these situations carefully, always making certain that you collect for every job you do. If someone fails to pay you promptly, stop doing work for them until all their outstanding bills are paid up. This will, at least, limit your losses and ensure that your woodworking business will be a financial success.

BUSINESS FORMS

The forms on the next three pages are slightly reduced versions of the original forms that can be used for your business. Included are a standard contract form used for many years and a specification addendum form for more complex jobs. Also included is a simple letterhead.

A. William Benitez Woodwork Services

402 Corral Lane   **447-4744**   **Austin, Texas 78745**

This is a very generic letterhead. You can use something like this or use stationery creation software, Word templates or some other program to create an attractive and original letterhead.

A.William Benitez Woodwork Services

402 Corral Lane   **447-4744**   **Austin, Texas 78745**

AGREEMENT FOR WOODWORK SERVICES Date:_____ This agreement is made as of the date above between A. William Benitez, a sole proprietor, and_____ of Austin, Texas 787___ , hereinafter called the Owner. For and in consideration of the mutual promises and covenants hereinafter set forth, the Owner and A. William Benitez agree as follows:

ARTICLE I: A. William Benitez will perform the work described herein:

_____
_____
_____
_____

ARTICLE II: The work shall be completed and installed as indicated above within 30 days of the execution of this agreement.

ARTICLE III: The Owner shall pay to A. William Benitez, in the manner described below, the total of $_____ plus $_____ sales tax for the work listed in Article I.

Total Price of the Work..$_____

Sales Tax...$_____
Total Price including Sales Tax.......................................$_____
Deposit: Due upon execution of agreement......................$_____
Balance: Payable in full upon completion of the work......$_____

ARTICLE IV: Additional items of agreement: Drawings and specifications attached.

ARTICLE V: Miscellaneous: A. William Benitez shall furnish all materials and labor for this work unless described to the contrary in Article I. All work shall be performed in a workmanlike manner to meet or exceed industry standards. This document and its attachments as listed in Article IV, constitute the entire agreement between the Owner and A. William Benitez, and it may be altered, amended, or repealed only by mutual agreement and a duly executed written instrument.

IN WITNESS WHEREOF, the Owner and A. William Benitez execute this Agreement as of the date stated above.

OWNER   **A. WILLIAM BENITEZ**

_____   _____

A William Benitez Woodwork Services

SPECIFICATIONS
ENTERTAINMENT CABINETS, BOOKCASES, AND KITCHEN CABINET DOORS:

For_____Address_____

_____

The following specifications shall apply to all the woodwork being done for this job. Additional notes listed below specifications shall also apply. These notes shall be added by mutual agreement prior to the execution of the contract.

- All units shall be constructed of ¾ inch maple plywood
- All exposed plywood edges shall be covered with solid wood edging or molding as shown in the drawings.
- All shelves except for VCR shelf shall be adjustable with brass standards and brass clips Brass standards shall be recessed to be flush with cabinet surfaces on all exposed areas.
- All unit doors shall be raised panel of solid maple with 2 ½ inch stiles and rails.
- During installation all units shall be trimmed to the walls.
- Doors shall be hinged with self closing, concealed euro hinges.
- TV space shall have a swivel pullout unit
- Component section shall have a pullout drawer for turntable.
- All drawers shall be constructed of ½ inch plywood with ¼ inch plywood bottoms except for the record drawer that will have a ½ inch plywood bottom.
- CD, record and tape drawers shall have appropriate plastic dividers.
- Doors in kitchen shall be standard stile and rail design except stiles and rails shall be 2 ½ inches wide and panel shall be standard glass adhered with clear silicone. These doors shall be hung with face frame mounted, self-closing euro hinges.

ADDITIONAL NOTES:

Eleven

Getting Help

The One-Person Business

A one-person business is your best course for financial success with low risk. This book is geared specifically to that form of business. There are many reasons to avoid hiring employees, not the least of which is that it can complicate your life and quite possibly take the joy out of your woodworking.

Hiring employees also creates a much more complex income tax situation and employees can increase your costs and your initial investment significantly. Obviously there will be times when you need some help because you have too much work or a job is too large to handle alone. Hiring subcontractors is a less complex way to deal with excess workloads.

What Is A Subcontractor?

While this is definitely an excellent way to handle more projects, don't believe you can subvert IRS payroll deduction requirements simply by calling someone a subcontractor. You can experience serious problems with the IRS if the term subcontractor is incorrectly defined. The IRS has certain requirements that must be met in order to consider someone a subcontractor. If you don't meet those requirements, your subcontractor will be considered an employee and you will be required to pay past due withholding and Social Security deductions plus penalties.

You can be safe by making certain the subcontractor is in business and has a business identity. That is, he or she has an address and phone number used for business and some past business experience with other customers. The subcontractor must also control his or her own hours.

If someone is working for you during certain hours that you control and you pay him or her on an hourly basis, that person is an employee. Calling him or her a subcontractor will not impress the IRS. If they check and find this kind of situation, they will believe this person is an employee and this will hurt you financially because you will have to pay past due payroll deductions that you did not collect.

Day Laborers

Naturally, if you only need someone for one day to help you install a cabinet or some similar work, you can hire a day laborer to help you and pay him or her for that day only without negative consequences.

In most communities there are places to pick up day laborers and this will usually work out fine. However, if you know someone or have a friend or coworker who can help you, this creates a much more comfortable work environment. Plus, you can leave this person at a customer's home without worrying about a stranger creating a problem for you.

Twelve

Simplifying While Maintaining Quality

Simplifying Is No Insult To Traditional Methods

Simplifying work methods can help you finish projects faster while still maintaining good quality. If you decide to make use of some simplified methods, it doesn't reflect in any way on traditional woodworking methods. Nor does it prevent you from using traditional methods for some of your work when a customer is prepared to pay for the extra time involved.

The main objective of simplifying methods is to help refine your woodworking skills to save time, make your work easier, and perhaps increase your profits. All of the methods described in this book are alternatives that are based on many years of experience and you may find them useful.

These alternative, simplified methods are not essential to making money with woodworking. However, they may facilitate faster completion of woodworking projects and this can lead to increased profits without sacrificing quality.

> *It may help you to better understand the concept of simpler methods if I discuss how these methods evolved for me and some of the basic techniques. Many years ago, when I started my woodworking business, it quickly became evident that it would be difficult for me to make a good living in my area using traditional woodworking methods.*

The time involved in building projects using the methods I had learned over the years tended to price me out of the market. It seemed that I either had to find faster methods or settle for a low wage and that was not acceptable to me.

I read a lot when I was starting out so I could learn as much possible. Over time it became clear that only a few woodworkers did well financially building projects using traditional methods. Some of these woodworkers had become well known in their area and others supplemented their income by writing books and creating videos about their work or endorsing products. It seemed to me that unless I could become this well known or famous, it was unlikely that I would be able to make a good living using traditional methods.

I decided to develop methods to complete my work faster and at a lower cost while still maintaining a high degree of quality. I began compiling ideas that would make things simpler and therefore faster. One of the major questions during this effort was, "What kind of joinery can I use on my furniture jobs?" This was an important question because mortise and tenon, dovetails, finger joints, dados, etc. comprise excellent joinery methods but I found them all time-consuming.

It became obvious to me that a strong, attractive, yet simple joinery method was essential for building furniture projects economically. Butt joints are simple and fast but have little strength so they weren't the answer.

My answer came when I found my first biscuit or plate joiner. Using this fine tool to reinforce the butt joints of various kinds proved to be a workable method for strong and attractive joinery.

This one tool helped me build beautiful projects quickly and easily without nail or screw holes to plug or fill. It takes a little effort to learn how to use a biscuit joiner effectively and efficiently but once learned, it will speed up your work and create strong joinery.

I never considered using dowels even though some woodworkers believe that dowels are a good alternative for other joinery methods. My own experience, and that of several other woodworkers, indicated that dowel joints are inherently weak because they lack adequate long grain glue surface. Dowels are round and most of their glue surfaces wind up against the end grain of boards. Glue does not adhere well to end grain. Therefore, the only part of the dowel that is actually holding is that portion that is glued to the long grain of the wood and this causes weak joints.

Many woodworkers mistakenly use dowels when gluing up boards to create a wide surface. This almost always causes joints to crack when the boards move and the dowels remain in place. In addition to these problems, they also make alignment of pieces difficult and time-consuming. Actually, when a set of boards are glued up properly to make a wide surface, the glue joint becomes stronger than the board itself. To test this yourself, glue up four or five pieces of boards six inches long and clamp them up. When the glue dries, hit the boards over a saw horse or some other hard surface until it breaks. It will always break in a board not the joint. Since the glue joint is stronger than the board, it is pointless to use dowels or anything else for any purpose except ease of alignment.

The Controversial Nails and Screws

Nails and screws offer an alternative for some cabinets such as those in kitchens. Screw holes can be plugged and nail holes filled. The combination of nails for assembly and screws for strength works well for many kitchens. However, this is definitely not the best answer for fine furniture. Although with shop made plugs it does give an acceptable appearance.

Using A System of Modules

Another way to save time and money building large projects is to build them in modules. This makes it easier to build the project in a small shop and often allows you to deliver and install furniture and cabinets without help.

> *Over the years, I have worked with many woodworkers. One of the most common mistakes they make is building large projects as one piece. I have seen entertainment centers that would barely fit through a doorway even when turned on the side and kitchen cabinet units that were over eight feet long. Some units were so heavy that it took six people to move.*

It is much simpler to build cabinets and furniture in modules that one person can carry. At worst, two people should be able to carry the biggest module. Building in this way makes the job much easier and facilitates the installation.

> *One of my contracts many years ago involved building all the cabinets for the data center of a large corporation's branch office. The units had to accommodate six people with their computers, storage and regular desk space. Plus, it included divider walls to afford limited privacy to the employees. The entire job was built at my shop. One person could carry each piece. The installation took two people because some of the cabinets had to be installed a few feet above the floor and a second person made the job easier but I could have done it alone. Once assembled, it appeared to be one large unit.*

The resistance to modules stems from the aversion to cabinets that seem to be assembled from a bunch of pieces. You can overcome this problem easily with good design features and a little care. First, make certain that the design gives the impression of one large piece. Secondly, assemble the modules in your shop to make certain everything fits properly. This way you can correct problems at the shop not on the job site. Don't wait till you get on site to find out that there is a problem with the modules fitting together.

Many years ago I built a very large entertainment center. It was constructed of MDF (Medium Density Fiberboard) covered with black, high gloss, plastic laminate. The unit included space for television and video recording equipment, plus a complete audio setup and some storage. The complete unit was 6' wide, 6' 6" tall and 26" deep. The extra two inches of depth beyond 24 were to accommodate a wire chase to hide the myriad of wires necessary for the various components. They could not be seen from inside or outside of the unit. The unit had casters so it could be moved from the wall for uncovering the wire chase and making changes.

Since the unit would be in three stacked modules covered by high gloss laminate, it was essential that the modules line up perfectly on site when they were assembled. I accomplished this by assembling the units at the shop without the laminate and using a belt sander to make certain that all the modules lined up at all points.

Once the MDF had been sanded into perfect alignment, I covered the outside surfaces with the high gloss black laminate and checked the final fit by assembling the modules. The completed unit looked like one large entertainment center with the joints almost invisible.

It was difficult for two people to carry the three modules because of the weight of the MDF with the laminate. It would have taken a large crew to move this cabinet as one unit. The completed unit took twelve carpet casters to roll easily and smoothly.

Take the time to design cabinets as modules. Make a sketch of the entire unit and then decide the best way to divide it into workable modules. Once this is decided, you can make the working drawings for the unit. Remember to divide the modules at the point that will be the least conspicuous so the finished appearance will give the impression of one unit.

If You Can't Hide It, Accentuate It

One last trick for building cabinets in modules involves the use of reveals. Sometimes it just isn't possible to assemble the modules so the unit appears as one large unit. In this case you do something to make the joints part of the design. One method that works well is to adjust the size of the cabinets to accommodate reveals. Make ¼-inch thick strips, place them between the modules, and recess them about ¼-inch. You can make these a different color as an accent but they work fine the same color as the project. The recess creates a shadow making the recess darker and it gives a very good appearance. It simply takes attention from the module joints by converting them to design features.

Finishing Methods

How you finish each of your projects is critically important. There are many different kinds of finishes and you probably have a favorite already. If your choice provides professional results that satisfy you and your customers, by all means continue to use it.

My favorite finish for natural wood is simply a clear coat. Before the clear coat, you can apply a stain. Wood stains come in many types and colors. I like the MinWax brand but there are many others. Most stains need to dry overnight before you can apply a clear coat but you can get water based stains that dry in one hour.

When selecting a stain color remember that it will look different depending on the color and grain of the wood. Your project may turn out a little darker or lighter than the sample that you saw in the store. Use a scrap piece to test the color. Before beginning, stir the stain thoroughly. The pigment has a tendency to settle to the bottom of the container. Using it without stirring will give a washed out and splotched look.

To prepare for staining, uniform sanding is critical. Sand the entire project evenly. Do not apply excessive pressure to a power sander during this job. Friction builds up when power sanding and if the sandpaper gets worn it will simply shine the surface instead of sanding it. These shiny spots will not take the stain well causing lighter areas on the surface. To avoid this, change sandpaper often and do not apply excessive pressure. It is a false economy to use sandpaper beyond its effective life.

Splotching appears on many wood surfaces. To avoid splotching, it often helps to apply a pre-stain coat. This can be mixed from your clear coat but it's best to keep things simple by purchasing a pre-stain product. Remember that this product will seal the wood slightly to keep the stain on the surface from splotching. This can cause the stain color to be lighter needing more than one coat.

Once the stain is applied, wipe off the excess with t-shirt rags. Wipe the surface completely making certain no streaks are left. If the stain dries before being wiped, the streaks can only be removed with paint or lacquer thinner and this will require additional staining.

After wiping, allow the stain to dry overnight, unless the instructions indicate otherwise. Do not sand the stained surface before applying the first coat of clear. Sanding at this time can cause unsightly lightened areas.

Once the stain is dry, apply a clear sanding sealer according to the instructions on the container. While you can simply apply a first coat of whatever clear coat product you are using, a sanding sealer will improve your finish, be easier to sand, and provide a better base for the last coat of clear finish.

After the sanding sealer dries completely, sand the surface by hand using a 400-grit sandpaper until the surface feels smooth as glass. Now you are ready to apply the final clear coat.

The clear coat should be brushed only with the grain of the wood and not over brushed. Just spread it as evenly as possible, thick enough so it will flow out but not so thick that it runs. When using fast drying clear coats, don't go back to brush completed areas because they will already be semi dry and brushing will leave deep and unsightly brush marks.

For some jobs a third coat may be a good idea. If you decide to apply another coat, sand exactly as you did previously before applying the next coat. For this last coat you can use a 600-grit sandpaper for a super smooth finish.

Bartley's Gel Varnish

There are many other readily available finishing products for cabinets and furniture. Bartley's Gel Varnish is an excellent but more time-consuming product. This product has many unique advantages. In addition to clear, it comes in various stain colors making it a combination stain and clear coat in a gel form. It can be applied with a brush or a rag and has a long open time making it easy to control. It has a six-hour drying time under normal conditions.

The most important advantage of Bartley's Gel Varnish is that it does not raise the grain of the wood when it is applied. One of the disadvantages is that it is priced considerably higher than other finishes and requires more coats to attain a semi-gloss finish.

Bartley's Gel Varnish is an excellent product for staining and finishing but not the best choice for a high gloss finish. Even after many coats it only attains a semi-gloss.

Deft Clear Wood Finish

This is an excellent, fast drying, clear coat product. It is basically a brushing lacquer that performs well if you follow the instructions carefully. Brush it on with a quality brush and allow it to flow out. It dries quite rapidly and it's critical not to go back and brush areas that have begun drying to avoid ugly brush marks that are impossible to remove without removing the entire finish. Another issue with Deft Clear Wood Finish is that it has a strong odor and vapors so it should be applied in a well ventilated area while wearing a respirator.

Deft does have a water based clear coat call Wood Armor. It works quite well but unlike Deft Wood Finish it doesn't work well in colder temperatures. It should be at least 65 degrees to apply this product.

Painting

Painting is another finishing option that works well for some projects. Small projects can be painted with spray cans. When spraying or brushing paint, always use a primer for the first coat and then sand all the surfaces smooth before applying a quality enamel. It is disappointing to see how many paint jobs are of obviously poor quality because there was no sanding between coats.

> *Years ago I built a complete kitchen for a customer who requested an unfinished job. Members of the family were going to apply the finish later. I advised the customer to allow me to finish the cabinets or at least accept my advice about how to get a good paint job. Instead members of the family applied the finish and obviously failed to properly prepare the surfaces. They didn't use a primer to seal the wood and there was no sanding between coats. The result was unattractive and the surfaces felt like sandpaper. The real issue for me was that when others were told I built the cabinets they might assume I also applied the finish.*

Spraying

The best and easiest to use tool for spraying wood cabinets and furniture with a clear coat is a HVLP (high volume low pressure) spray unit. However, spraying has its complexities and safety issues. There is a learning curve required for properly using a spray gun even though some think it is just point and shoot. Before starting to spray actual jobs, practice on various surfaces to get the feel for it and to see how the finish falls on the surface. This practice will help you become proficient at spraying.

With all finishes you must consider harmful vapors and flammability. This is especially true of lacquer finishes. Avoid spraying lacquer unless you have a safe and properly ventilated area to finish your projects. And always wear the correct respirator for the finish being used.

In addition to good ventilation and a high quality respirator, make certain your equipment is designed so it doesn't cause sparks that could set off the combustible sprayed lacquer. I strongly suggest that you learn how to use lacquer products properly and safely before spraying any projects with them.

Also consider the regulations in your community regarding the use of lacquer sprays. In some areas you must have a specially designed spray booth to legally spray lacquer. Check local regulations to avoid problems with local code enforcement.

Thirteen

Safety

Safety is the most important topic in this book and it is definitely in your best interest to read and adhere to these safety rules. If you are a long time woodworker and still have all your fingers and body parts, it probably isn't by accident. Most likely it is because you have a healthy respect for the rules of safety and you realize the importance of giving every power tool your full and undivided attention before turning it on.

POWER TOOLS ARE INHERENTLY DANGEROUS! Any tool that can cut wood can also cut skin and bone. Please keep this in mind every time you use a power tool. Here are a few more simple suggestions that will help you avoid injuries:

- Plan every cut carefully before starting the tool. This is a common oversight by many woodworkers. Instead of just jumping in and starting the cut, decide exactly what you are going to do and what problems might pose themselves during the procedure.
- Clamp work pieces securely before cutting, routing, or sanding. It is much quicker and easier to just hold the piece down with your hands while making the cut or routing the edge but you are definitely increasing the risk of injury.
- Read and adhere to the safety guidelines that came with the power tool. These guidelines are written to help you avoid serious injuries. It only takes a few minutes to read through the small booklets that come with power tools today. You might learn a little something that will help you stay safe.

- If you are using a power tool with one hand, always check the location of the other hand before starting the tool. This may sound silly but it is a good way to keep all your fingers. If you are cutting with a tool in one hand, a moment could ensure that your other hand is in a safe place where it will be clear even from kickbacks.
- Another part of planning is to visualize the complete procedure before you start. This will help you avoid potential kickback or other injury causing incidents.
- Never use power tools if you are tired, taking medications or using alcohol or drugs. This is a sure way to get hurt.
- Never use a power tool while someone is talking to you or distracting you in some way. It only takes a split second for a serious injury to change your life. If someone interrupts your cut, stop cutting and tell them not to speak to you while you are using a power tool.
- Always use ear and eye protection and dust masks when using power tools.

Woodworking is an enjoyable hobby and it can be profitable as a business. Don't let a moment of carelessness ruin it for you. Think before turning on any power tool and take good care of yourself and others around you.

SPECIAL NOTE ON TABLE SAWS: The table saw is probably the most commonly used stationary power tool for woodworking. It's a tool that has many diverse uses. With the right kind of jigs and fixtures it can perform amazingly well and produce an almost infinite variety of cuts. It is also involved in more than ninety percent of shop injuries. These machines can injure you seriously.

Using a table saw requires your total attention. In addition to the potential for cutting you, when improperly used, a table saw is capable of throwing pieces of materials back at astounding speed. These pieces can cause serious injuries by striking you in various locations.

This information is not meant to frighten you but to make certain that you fully understand the power of a table saw. Always give your work on the table saw your full attention.

Take the time to learn the safety rules for your machine and adhere to them. It only takes one mistake to cause a serious injury that can affect your life for many years to come. Please be careful.

> ***Note:*** *If your budget allows, consider the SawStop Table Saws. These units are specially designed so the blade stops instantly and retracts below the table when it contacts skin to avoid serious injuries. It also has a riving knife to protect against kickbacks. Get more information and view a video at the SawStop web site at: http://www.sawstop.com.*

Fourteen

The Order Of Things

As you complete more jobs for your customers it will become clear that the order in which certain things are done is important. It can help you work safer and more efficiently.

Doing things in the best possible order requires a high degree of attentiveness. Devoting your full attention to your own safety, the needs of your customers, and the overall quality of every job will contribute much to your success in the woodworking business.

What follows is a long list of basic rules with explanations and they apply equally to your safety and to any tasks you may be doing for yourself or a customer.

Think About What You Are Doing

This certainly sounds obvious but so many times a person is thinking about a dozen other things besides what he or she is doing. If you are fortunate, failure to follow this rule may only lead to a mistake, but it could just as easily lead to serious injury.

Measure Twice And Cut Once

That old saying "Measure twice and cut once," is an example of rule one. When you are thinking about what you are doing, you will take the second measurement to be certain it is correct before actually cutting the wood. While this is always important, it can be critical when you have calculated your materials closely without consideration for waste. By taking the time to think, you will avoid ruining a piece of material that you really need to complete the work.

Visualize The Task Through To Completion

This sounds difficult and time consuming to some because they are always in a rush to get things done, but it's really simple. Just take a few seconds to imagine how the cut will proceed so you can prepare for potential difficulties.

This could help you realize that a certain crosscut on a table saw may cause a kickback or you are about to run a router in the wrong direction possibly damaging a surface. Common problems are diminished in size when you are ready for them and visualization prepares you for whatever actually happens.

Where Are My Hands?

Some think this rule is silly because it seems so obvious. Unfortunately, we sometimes overlook the obvious and this can be dangerous. When you are about to start a power tool capable of causing serious injury, it is critical to know the exact location of your hands before a motor is started. Once the tool starts, it could be too late.

Perform The Task

Once the first four rules are done it's time to get the task completed. Now you will proceed with the full knowledge that the task will be performed accurately and safely.

Put The Tool Down Carefully

Once the task is performed you may still be standing there with the tool in one or both hands. Now is the time to turn off the tool, give it time to stop fully, and put it down on the floor or on a bench safely. If it is a stationary power tool it is important to completely finish the cut, turn off the machine, and wait for it to come to a complete stop.

A Time-Consuming Process?

All this sounds like it could be time consuming and it does take a little time. Obviously, you won't be able to work as fast while taking these steps. This doesn't necessarily mean that your projects are going to take longer. Remember that these steps will help you avoid mistakes that can take many hours to correct. More importantly, it can help you avoid serious injuries that can take months or even years to overcome.

Assembling In The Right Order

The best order of things can come to you while assembling a project. Two examples of how carefully determining the best order of things can help you appear below.

The biscuit joiner is my favorite joinery tool so I am often assembling cabinets and furniture using biscuit wafers. This requires putting glue into the slots cut by the biscuit joiner prior to the actual assembly of the unit. Early on I realized that the order in which I put the glue and the biscuits in the slots was important.

The first time I proceeded with an assembly without thinking it through and visualizing the procedure, I wound up with slots full of glue being turned upside down and dripping glue on my project and my work surface. After that first time I planned carefully by thinking and visualizing and the only slots that were ever upside down had a biscuit in them so the glue could not drip out. This may not be important to some, but being a basically neat worker the glue mess was a problem for me.

Another time when thinking saved me a lot of unpleasantness involved spray painting. Years ago when I built a set of lecterns for a hotel, I sprayed clear lacquer over stain. On the first batch I made the mistake of assembling them completely before spraying and quickly found out that spraying into enclosed spaces caused the overspray to come right back at me in large and unpleasant quantities. It was a lesson I never forgot.

Recently, while building new kitchen cabinets for my own home, I decided to spray paint them. Since the cabinets are an off-white acrylic enamel, I used an airless spray unit that atomizes the paint. Remembering the lesson that I had previously learned as I visualized how the spray job would go, I decided to leave the backs off of the cabinets and spray them separately. This worked out great as it allowed the sprayed enamel to pass through the cabinet as I was painting the inside instead of coming back at me after hitting the back. I found it a more pleasant experience and I believe a better paint job without the excess overspray.

Sometimes, a failure to think and visualize causes a painful situation that ensures you will do both next time. One tool that can teach this lesson promptly is the pneumatic nailer.

Although I am a careful person, sometimes things just happen. Once, while using a pneumatic finish nailer to assemble a project, I held one piece with one hand while pressing the other in close for nailing. I had my fingers too close and when I pressed the trigger to shoot the nail it came out the side of the material and directly into my finger right to the bone.

The pain was excruciating and I bled considerably all over the cabinet. I had the wound checked out and everything was fine but it was an excellent lesson and since then my fingers have never been within range of a nail so it has never been repeated. Thinking and visualizing how that nail could go would have saved me the pain and possibly more serious injury. Plus, I would not have had to sand the blood off my cabinet.

The woodworking business requires planning and organization to decide what, when, and how you are going to do things. It's also important to remember that the order of carrying out these functions may make your work safer, faster, and even cleaner. So, spend time thinking and visualizing before doing.

Fifteen

Everyday Lessons

In the woodworking business you will be handling various jobs and working with many customers. This chapter describes many situations to point out some of the possibilities and how best to handle them. All of them were real jobs and involved the specific projects described with drawings, photos, or both.

Learn From These Situations

Please take the time to read about the jobs and notice how they were handled and why various steps were taken. This should help prepare you for some of the customer situations you may face in your own business.

Remember, these situations were handled in a certain way for a specific customer and use that information but don't be bound by the methods. You could come up with a better way to handle any situation and it's important not to close yourself to that possibility.

Drawings

The drawings shown here were not made up for this book. They are all original drawings for real jobs. This isn't the only way to prepare drawings and your drawing technique may be better. If so, that is what you should use for your drawings. The important thing is that drawings fulfill their purpose of clarifying the work for both parties to a contract for woodworking.

Customer With Few Design Ideas

The first job involves a large entertainment center that was built into a recess in a living room wall. This customer had various components to be housed by an entertainment center but only a limited concept of the design beyond it fitting into the recessed wall. The woodworker had to use the few details furnished by the customer to come up with a workable design that incorporated the requested features and then prepare a price for the job. This job lent itself perfectly to working with modules and was built in nine pieces.

It was a somewhat complex job that involved solid oak, raised panel doors, European hinges, and pocket hinges that allowed the TV doors to move completely out of sight. To the right and left of the TV space were open shelves to accommodate knick knacks. It also had speaker cloth over some of the doors to accommodate hidden speakers and several drawers for CDs, DVDs and other media.

Since there were so many modules, the unit was pre-assembled completely in the shop to make certain everything would fit on site. The owner was completely satisfied even though she had little to contribute to the original design of the cabinet. You will run into many customers who have a general idea of what they want but no specific design ideas. It's your job to help them visualize clearly what you will be delivering. Take as much time as necessary to make certain they understand your drawings and specifications.

Customer Who Knows Exactly What He Or She Wants

The exact opposite of the previous customer is one who has most of the design worked out in advance before calling you. They may even have a drawing or you may have to draw up the details but you will have little latitude regarding design with customers like this. The one piece entertainment center below was designed entirely by the customer and it was built to his exact specifications.

Both jobs involve entertainment centers but the process is completely different because of the way you have to work with the customer. To satisfy both you must be willing to listen and understand what the customer wants.

Remember that you are the expert. There are times when you will run into a customer who has an idea that simply will not work because it would be structurally unsound. It's your job to guide them to a design that resembles what he or she wants while being workable. This is critically important.

Many years ago I befriended a local woodworker who regularly called me for advice. One day he called me to see a job that was giving him problems. The job involved a built-in TV cabinet that was divided into a top section to accommodate a large TV entertainment center combo. This top section had a roll top that opened to expose the TV combo unit.

The bottom part of the cabinet was a chest of drawers divided into two sections of large drawers with a partition between them. This partition obviously served to support the weight of the large TV combo unit. After he completed the cabinet, the customer asked him to make the bottom two drawers into one large wide drawer to accommodate rifles while still maintaining the appearance of two drawers so the cabinet would not look strange.

Making this work required cutting through the center cabinet partition between the drawers. My friend did as he was asked and created the large drawer. It seem to work fine until the TV unit was put in place and then the weight of the unit caused the center to sag because it was no longer supported by the center partition. It no longer looked good and caused the drawers to bind. He wanted me to help him resolve the problem.

I explained to him that the only solution was to either go back to two bottom drawers by replacing the partition or rebuild the entire cabinet with a reinforced section to support the weight of the TV unit without depending on the center partition between the drawers. I told him that removing the center partition was a serious design error and he responded that it was what the customer wanted. He couldn't see that as the expert it was his job to convince the customer the change could not be made without rebuilding the unit.

The woodworker had to rebuild the cabinet and took a financial loss. As it turned out he had made several errors; his drawings were inadequate, there was no contract, and he had received no deposit. So, in addition to executing a bad design, he lost money on the job. You can avoid this by learning your craft and being the expert.

Adjusting Grades Of Furniture To Situations

Some of your projects will be quite elegant and expensive looking but others may be plain. Customers have different needs and you should be ready to give them what they want. That doesn't indicate a willingness to cut quality. You never want to build anything you wouldn't want others to see. However, you can build low-cost alternatives for customers.

Some customers want elegant furniture for a living or dining room and you want to fulfill those needs. Naturally, those jobs cost more so make certain the customer understands why the costs are higher and deliver a flawless job that will be shown off proudly.

That is how a reputation is built. Once you have been in business for a while most of your customers will come to you as referrals from other jobs. But all of those customers don't have to be people desiring elegant cabinets and furniture. You may also be called on by those who need attractive, functional, and reasonably priced units that will serve them well. These are also good jobs.

An example of such a customer was one who had just added a bed-room to her small home for her teenage son. As it turned out the room was quite small and had no closet. She wanted an armoire so he could have hanging clothes and a drawer for folded clothes.

When one hears the word armoire it almost always summons up a picture of an expensive antique but that isn't what she had in mind and her budget was quite limited so it was a challenge to this wood-worker.

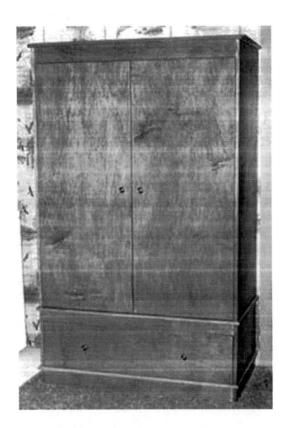

The armoire above was built from an inexpensive grade of plywood and served the teenager well. The top section opened to expose a generous space with a rod for hanging clothes. The large drawer at the bottom was quite deep and easily handled his folded clothes. It was an inexpensive solution to the problem and the customer was quite pleased with it even though it certainly wasn't elegant.

Small Simple Jobs

Accepting small simple jobs will help you to gain customers who may someday call you for much larger jobs. It is also a great way to improve your skills. Small jobs are most often less demanding and help you learn to calculate reasonable prices for your work. It's a good path to valuable experience. What follows are just a few small jobs that were completed over the years. With some, the drawings are also included, with others just the photos. In all cases a few details are included.

Coffee And End Tables

The photo of the coffee table appears below and the drawings appear on the next page. They were intended as a set with an attractive, somewhat southwest look with a surface that would not need coasters to protect it from drinks.

Notice that the surface of the table is tile. Originally it was made with a plastic laminate surface but the customer thought it looked cheap and she was right. By adding a small, raised trim to the design and installing tile on the surface, the appearance of the table was improved dramatically and satisfied the customer fully. The original drawings appear below.

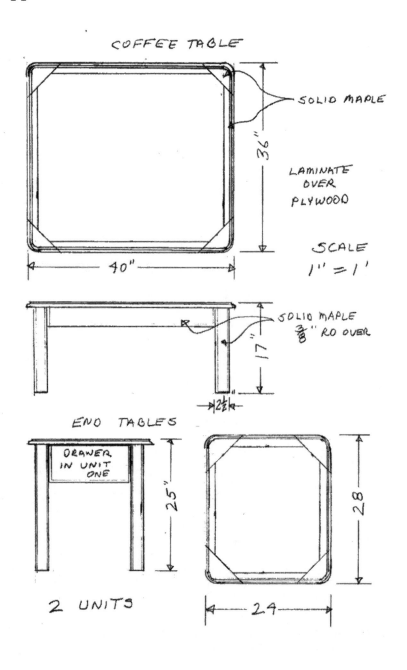

Notice that it is a simple, straight forward design but as you can see on the end table at left and the coffee table on page 133, it was significantly improved by the tile surface.

There will be times you will have to change a design to satisfy a customer. How you handle this determines if the customer becomes an asset to your marketing or a detriment. It may be necessary to charge a customer more for changes but it is worth giving them as much consideration as possible if they are reasonable with you. Keep an open mind when resolving these issues and you will gain customers.

End Table/Desk Combo

Sometimes you will have to combine projects. The piece below was built for a customer who wanted a combination end table and desk in the bedroom.

The molding and finish on this piece had to match the existing headboard with what could be considered a streaked stain. Normally stains should be smooth and even but this had to be done differently to meet the customer's requirements. Below are the drawings for this End Table/Desk Combo.

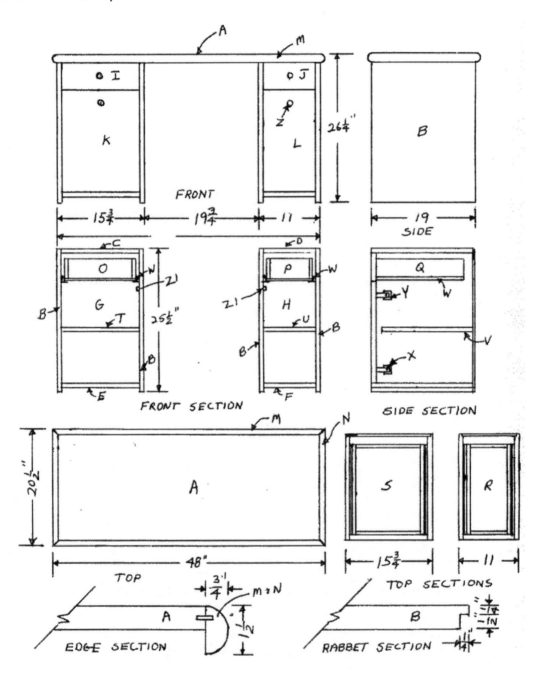

Glass Top Table

You may run into interesting jobs like this one. The customer had a large piece of ½ inch thick glass that she wanted to use for a table. As an additional requirement, the floor in the home was made of long leaf pine flooring that was quite old. They wanted the table to be built of long leaf pine to fit in with the floor. The woodworker was able to find enough long leaf pine to build the table and came up with a design to meet the customer's needs. A photo of the table appears below.

The glass was accommodated by a solid long leaf pine frame with the outside edges rounded over. On this job it was important to have a somewhat Southwest look to tie in with the chairs they already had. The legs were constructed by gluing up three thicknesses of long leaf pine and then planing them and rounding the corners. The apron was made from a single thickness of the same material with the bottom edge rounded over and several decorative drillings. Notice how well it blends in with the floor fulfilling the customers request.

Bathroom Or Foyer Mirror And Table

Another project that involved using an existing piece of glass is the mirror frame below. This was just a small mirror with beveled edges that wound up being used first as a bathroom mirror and then as part of an entry furniture set. It was a simple oak frame with rabbets to accommodate the mirror. The rabbet had to be cut narrower than normal to avoid hiding the bevel edge of the mirror, an attractive feature the customer wanted to remain visible.

The photo above shows the mirror in a bathroom setting and the photo on the right shows the same mirror set vertically in an entry way.

On the next page are the original drawings for the entry table which was basically a solid oak table with tapered legs. The drawings include a simple jig that was used to cut the tapers. The apron was also solid oak and the drawings include details about the angles used to assemble the table. The top was basically an oak frame with a decorative edge around a fire agate color plastic laminate over plywood.

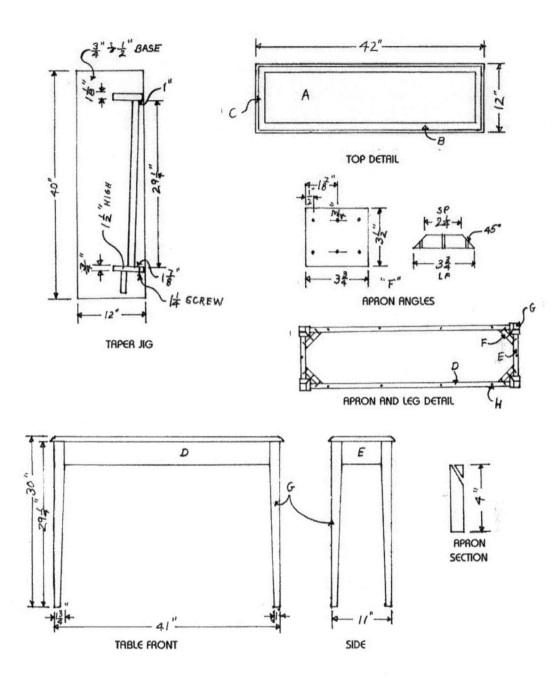

While the mirror frame was a simple project, there were many ways to do the job. The drawings on the next page not only show the way the frame was actually constructed but also other options that may be used to create a frame using an existing mirror. It also shows various ways to create a rabbet for the mirror.

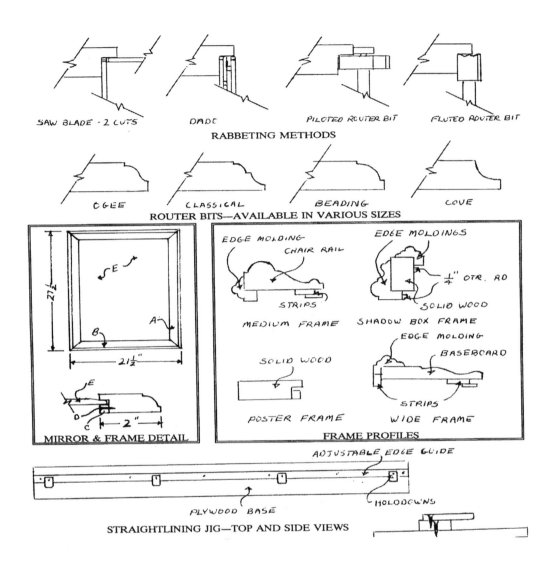

SAW BLADE - 2 CUTS   DADE   PILOTED ROUTER BIT   FLUTED ROUTER BIT

RABBETING METHODS

OGEE   CLASSICAL   BEADING   COVE

ROUTER BITS—AVAILABLE IN VARIOUS SIZES

MIRROR & FRAME DETAIL   FRAME PROFILES

STRAIGHTLINING JIG—TOP AND SIDE VIEWS

Laundry Cabinet

The laundry cabinet that appears on the next page is one of those completely functional jobs. When working with cabinets for laundry rooms it's important to avoid taking things for granted. Check the job out carefully making certain that the washing machine and dryer doors do not interfere with the installation. Take careful measurements anytime cabinets fit between two walls and especially in a small space. It's critical to allow space on both sides to accommodate easy installation.

The photo above was difficult to take because the utility room was too small to accommodate a full view. You can tell in the left side of the photo that there is a matching scribe that covers a space on each side of the cabinet. This makes the installation easier and leaves an attractive appearance. Check the drawings on the next page for a clearer view of this scribe.

This cabinet was constructed entirely of paint grade maple plywood even though it was simply finished with a clear coat. The doors were edged with maple veneer and installed using totally concealed European hinges made by Blum. The shelves are adjustable. Notice that the cabinet is not normal depth to avoid interfering with the top loading washer door.

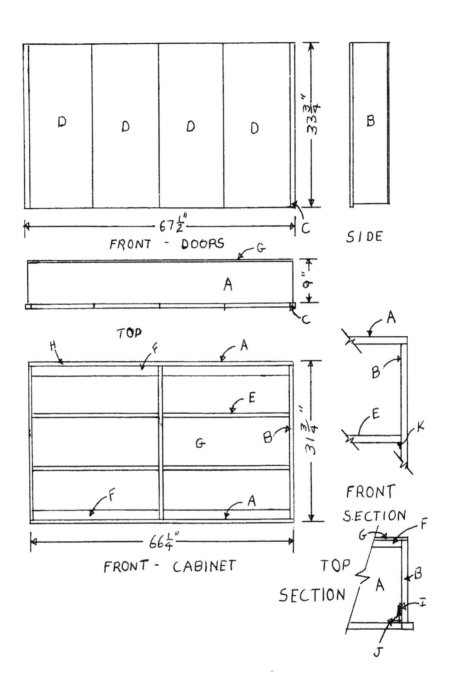

Laundry Room Cabinet Drawings

Drawings For A Large Job

The next four pages contain original drawings from a large job done many years ago. They are old and did not reproduce well.

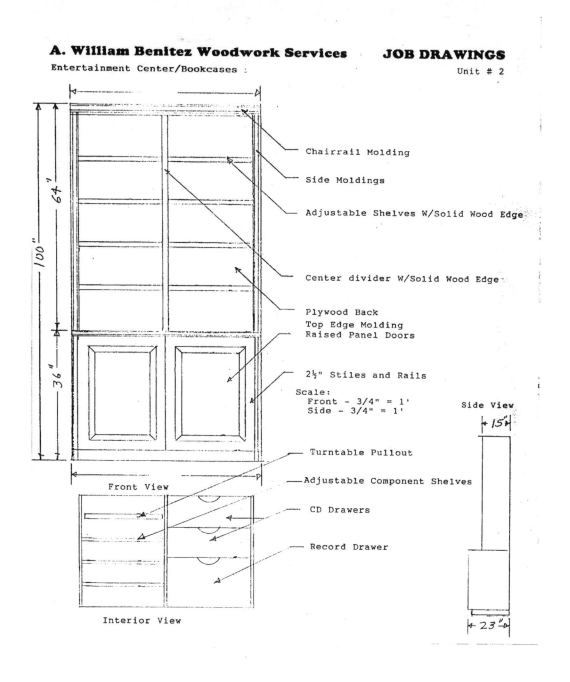

A. William Benitez Woodwork Services   **JOB DRAWINGS**

Entertainment Center/Bookcases :   Unit # 2

Chairrail Molding

Side Moldings

Adjustable Shelves W/Solid Wood Edge

Center divider W/Solid Wood Edge

Plywood Back
Top Edge Molding
Raised Panel Doors

2½" Stiles and Rails

Scale:
   Front - 3/4" = 1'
   Side - 3/4" = 1'

Side View

Front View

Turntable Pullout

Adjustable Component Shelves

CD Drawers

Record Drawer

Interior View

This job involved two entertainment/bookcase combo units and one full bookcase unit. Notice that the drawings were presented on letterhead type pages and that everything is clearly marked as originally requested by the customer.

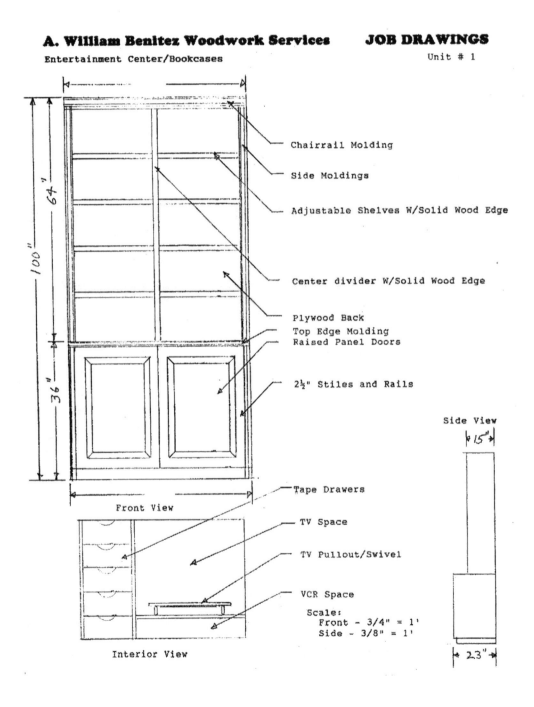

A. William Benitez Woodwork Services   **JOB DRAWINGS**

Entertainment Center/Bookcases   Unit # 1

Chairrail Molding

Side Moldings

Adjustable Shelves W/Solid Wood Edge

Center divider W/Solid Wood Edge

Plywood Back
Top Edge Molding
Raised Panel Doors

2½" Stiles and Rails

Side View

Front View

Tape Drawers

TV Space

TV Pullout/Swivel

VCR Space

Scale:
   Front - 3/4" = 1'
   Side - 3/8" = 1'

Interior View

This is the drawing of the bookcase unit. Again the details are complete so almost anyone can understand them. Even though they didn't reproduce well, it was decided that the original drawings would be of more value to you than redrawing them.

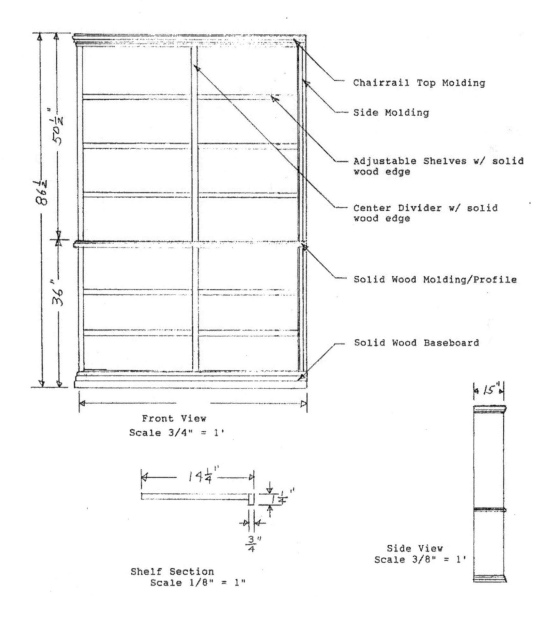

A. William Benitez Woodwork Services   **JOB DRAWINGS**

BOOKCASE UNIT   Unit # 3

Chairrail Top Molding

Side Molding

Adjustable Shelves w/ solid wood edge

Center Divider w/ solid wood edge

Solid Wood Molding/Profile

Solid Wood Baseboard

Front View
Scale 3/4" = 1'

Shelf Section
Scale 1/8" = 1"

Side View
Scale 3/8" = 1'

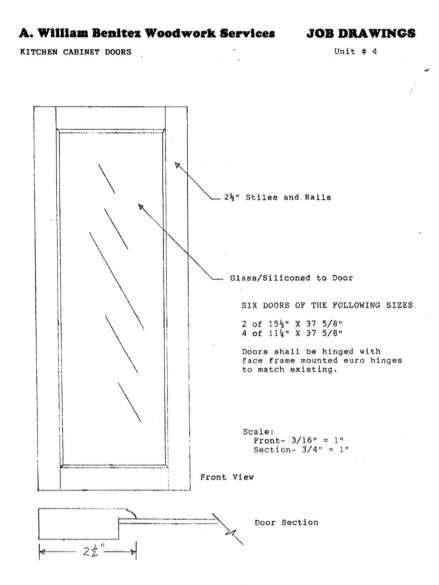

A. William Benitez Woodwork Services   **JOB DRAWINGS**

KITCHEN CABINET DOORS   Unit # 4

$2\frac{1}{2}$" Stiles and Rails

Glass/Siliconed to Door

SIX DOORS OF THE FOLLOWING SIZES

2 of $15\frac{1}{2}$" X 37 5/8"
4 of $11\frac{1}{4}$" X 37 5/8"

Doors shall be hinged with
face frame mounted euro hinges
to match existing.

Scale:
  Front- 3/16" = 1"
  Section- 3/4" = 1"

Front View

$2\frac{1}{2}$"

Door Section

Another part of this job involved replacing six upper kitchen cabinet doors with glass doors. This drawing describes how these would be done in clear details so the customer could be confident in the work to be performed in the kitchen.

This set of drawings accompanied job specifications and a contract that described the work, referred to these drawings, and requested a fifty percent deposit upon execution of the contract. The customer accepted the contract and made the check that day.

Final Lessons For Success

Respecting your customers is one of the main keys to success and it is often overlooked. That is unfortunate because financial success rests on your customers. Good woodworking skills are important but if you can't sell those skills to prospective customers there is no profit and without profit you won't succeed financially.

If you respect and value all your customers, the time will come when your reputation will completely prevent the need for advertising your business. People will seek you out and willingly pay you more than other woodworkers.

The drawings on the previous four pages are an example of this. I was called to this home based on the recommendation of a neighbor for whom I had done work. I spent a couple of hours with the prospect discussing exactly what he wanted and then I went home and made these drawings. I calculated the pricing and prepared all the documentation including the contract.

A couple of days later I returned and presented my documentation and spent time carefully explaining every detail of how I would do the job using the drawings to clarify any questions. An hour later I left there with a signed contract and a check for the deposit.

I completed the work and installed all the cabinets exactly as shown on the drawings. I spent most of a day on the job to install all the cabinets and replace the upper kitchen cabinet doors. While I worked, the customer visited with me several times when he brought me tea and water. During one of those times he confided in me that my price was considerably higher than the next bid but after seeing the professionalism of my documents and listening to my presentation, he could not give the work to anyone else regardless of the price.

It's not really that difficult to value your customers. The first step is to always follow the golden rule. Consider how you would like to be treated under the same circumstances and act accordingly.

To find out what someone really wants, start by really listening. That may sound simple but it should be fairly obvious to you that most people are mentally busy calculating what they are going say next instead of listening. Put yourself in a better position to get more work by really listening to your prospects.

Don't be condescending. Just because you are the expert is no reason to talk down to prospects. After all, they are the ones who must choose you if you are to succeed. When prospects sense condescension they may simply contract with someone else. Prospects want to hire you because you have valuable skills, not to be insulted because they don't share those skills.

When you go to see a job, listen carefully and take copious notes. You can't get too much information. The more you know about the job and the customer the more likely you are to deliver exactly what the customer wants. Use all that information to prepare detailed drawings and specifications that help to avoid misunderstandings. You don't need perfect, architectural quality drawings, but they must be clear, concise, and easy for the prospect to understand. When questions about the drawings or documents come up, answer them promptly and completely to engender the trust of prospects.

Once this trust develops, the prospect will become a customer. If you then follow-up by delivering everything you promised and perhaps even more, the customer will become an advertisement for your business to all his or her friends, family, and business associates. This is invaluable to the financial success of your business.

Sixteen

Final Notes From Bill

After more than twenty-five years of doing almost every kind of woodworking project, there are few things in this business that I have not experienced. Now that I have retired from woodworking to writing and publishing, books like this one give me the opportunity to share my first hand experiences and help others.

This last chapter includes a few final notes I believe you may find valuable. In addition to these notes, I welcome hearing about your own experiences and any questions that come up for you in the woodworking business. Please email be at: bill@woodworking-business.com and I will respond as promptly as possible. Thanks again for purchasing this book.

Become An Expert

To be really profitable it helps to be a recognized expert in the woodworking field. Strive to be the best woodworker in your area. That's not as difficult as it may seem. Look around and see how many people really excel at their chosen profession.

Over the years I've found that most people, including woodworkers, simply do little more than what is absolutely required. Some actually work hard to avoid doing what is obviously the right thing. There are a few people who excel but for the most part, mediocrity reigns supreme. With a little effort, you will easily place yourself in the top five percent of woodworkers and get paid accordingly.

Develop Your Communication Skills

Those in the top five percent of their field are in demand and are paid the most. What does it take to be in that top five percent? There are two very basic things you must do to attain that status. First, you must have or develop good communications skills. That means being able to get your message across clearly to everyone, especially potential customers. Those skills put you head and shoulders above most other woodworkers.

If you don't have those skills, work to improve your vocabulary and your communications skills. There are colleges, adult education programs and even home study courses to help you with this. If there is a toastmaster's club near you, join it to improve your rapport with the public.

Are you wondering what this has to do with woodworking? Well, it has little to do with woodworking skills but a lot to do with succeeding financially using your woodworking or any other skills. Getting people to choose you and even pay you more than other woodworkers is essential to your success and your communications skills will help you can get your message across.

Never Stop Learning About Woodworking

The second thing is to learn everything you can about woodworking. The worse thing you can do is stop learning and assume you know everything necessary to succeed in your business. It's not enough to know how to build a few things. Be ready for bigger jobs as time progresses. Learn from every job, from every other woodworker, from magazines, and even furniture stores. Fill your mind with new ideas on how to build things.

When you are visiting a furniture store, study the furniture in detail. You will be surprised how many great ideas will come to you from studying even cheap furniture that you would not consider buying. Not that you will use their methods but something will make you think and could lead to some really useful information.

Go to trade shows and talk with other woodworkers. Learn what others are doing and how and why they are doing those things. Find out if these methods will work for you. Or, perhaps they can serve as the basis for new methods of your own. Don't just accept existing methods as the end all. Create your own way of doing things. Think about how to make things better, faster, easier. Learn how to help your potential customers design exactly what they want or need and show them the best way to do it. You will have to visualize the project and explain clearly and exactly how you will create it.

Use Drive Time To Learn

You will probably be driving to various locations to bid jobs. Instead of spending that time listening to news or music or letting your mind chatter away, listen to motivational tapes. There are many good ones on the market. Wayne Dyer has some excellent tapes. Earl Nightingale, who died many years ago, had many excellent tapes. His tape or CD set entitled **Lead The Field** is excellent. You can probably get a copy from the Conant Company or at some used bookstore. These tapes or CDs help to instill the values that are important to anyone, but especially to small business owners.

Visualize And Share Your Vision With Customers

Do you believe that as the expert your only responsibility is to build and deliver a product to your customers without detailed explanations. Even if customers won't understand all the details, they deserve basic details about how you will do the job and why one thing works better than another. If you approach your prospects with the attitude of, "I'm the expert and I always know the best way to build things," you should consider getting over yourself.

Customers like people who try to explain things even if they don't really understand. It gives them a feeling that you care what they think and they would be better off dealing with you even if it means paying more than the lower bid. Be an expert who helps people to understand your work and they will flock to you and pay your prices without complaint.

Always Go The Extra Mile

Go the extra mile for all your customers. Don't nickel and dime them for small items. Price your work so you don't need to sweat the small stuff. Never make promises you can't keep. Always deliver what and when you say you will. If a serious problem arises and you can't deliver exactly on time, contact your customer as soon as you know about the problem. Don't wait until the last minute and just not show up. Treat every customer as the most important people in your business. Be confident and positive with your customers because it builds trust.

Never criticize your competition to a potential customer. Sell yourself and your work in a positive way. If your competitor is doing poor work, his reputation will follow him. Mentioning or dwelling on the quality of a competitor's work will just diminish your rapport with a customer.

Remember the Golden Rule

Treat everyone as you would like to be treated. If an unpleasant situation arises and you don't know exactly how to respond to it, stop and reflect on the situation before you act. Then act as you would like to be treated if you were on the other end of the situation. This will always result in action that is best for your customer and your business. The result of these decisions will also be mentioned to other potential customers.

Stay Positive

Maintain a positive attitude. Sometimes this is hard to do but it helps you do the best possible job. Know your limitations but be ready to learn and expand your knowledge to overcome those limitations. A positive state of mind will help your health and your business. Most customers dislike doing business with negative people. Fear and doubt can overwhelm almost anyone if allowed to do so and such fears are felt by potential customers who will doubt that you can deliver as promised. This could cause them to hesitate and find another woodworker.

Avoid Grief On Your Jobs Whenever Possible

It may seem strange for this topic to follow staying positive and come right before loving your work but it is the perfect place for it. Some of you may find this topic unfair to prospects for your work or perhaps funny, but it is quite serious. If you love woodworking, the customers you work for could definitely impact your feelings about the woodworking business.

While it is important to always deal with your prospects and customers fairly and with respect, you will run into customers who can best be described as impossible to please. The good thing is that it isn't that difficult to recognize them before you get a job. What you do when you recognize a really troublesome potential customer could affect your peace of mind.

To enjoy your work as much as possible it is best to avoid customers who will not appreciate your efforts to do a good job for them. Here are a few clues that will help you recognize one of those prospects who could become one of these unpleasant customers while you are checking out the job.

- These prospects will complain about every other person who has ever done work for them. From their conversation it will seem that no one has ever treated them with respect.
- No matter how competitive your pricing, they will try everything imaginable to lower your price even more.
- They will almost certainly resist the deposit vehemently reminding you of everyone who has cheated them in the past.
- Nothing will be easy and most of your ideas will be dismissed.
- You will have to spend a great deal more time with them then you spend with most prospects and usually that time will not be pleasant.

Once you have identified one of these prospects a decision must be made as to whether you really want to do the job at any price. You are then faced with choosing from two possibilities.

- The first is to avoid getting the job by telling the prospect that you no longer take that kind of work. Or, you could say that you are overwhelmed with work and they should call someone else or try you again in six months.
- The second possibility is to give the prospect an exceptionally high quote. In which case, they may reject the quote and you won't have to deal with doing the job. Or, you will get the job and you will be paid extra for putting up with the grief. The problem with the second choice is that you may get the job and even though you make good money the unpleasantness may be difficult to take.

My way to avoid doing these jobs was giving extremely high quotes and it almost always worked. I did have a couple of really unpleasant customers over my many years in the business but the high quote usually got me out of doing the job.

I remember one unpleasant prospect who called me for a complete kitchen cabinet job many years ago. I spent almost two hours with her discussing every detail of what she wanted in her kitchen and by the time I left it was clear that I did not want her job at any price. I did calculate what I would normally charge for the job and then I doubled that figure. I went back two days later and gave her the quote and she was obviously shocked and did not give me the job. Perhaps that wasn't a nice thing to do but my peace of mind has always been important to me and I honestly believed that doing a job for her would have a negative impact on my enjoyment of my work.

When it comes to potentially unpleasant customers, you have to make the decision. You may decide not to risk losing business even if a job may be unpleasant. Or, you may prefer to totally avoid such jobs. It's your business so you must make the decision that is right for you.

The Work You Love

If you goal is to make your living doing work you really enjoy, the woodworking business can offer a great opportunity for that. Woodworking is creative and challenging and offers the potential for a good living. However, don't go into this business if you have serious security issues and need a secure income and regular benefits to live comfortably. Persons with those needs should find a job that offers such security to maintain peace of mind.

Risk is always a part of running your own small business. Before leaving a job to jump into woodworking full time, you must love this work enough to accept some risks. If you aren't certain, you can still start woodworking on a part-time basis until your confidence grows.

Finally, remember that the woodworking business is seldom an opportunity to become wealthy. What you can do is make a good living and have a life filled with satisfying work and the joy of doing work you really love. That is much more than many people ever attain. Good Luck.

Glossary

Accounting: a precise record of the financial transactions of your business.

Accounting Software: software used to maintain information on the financial transactions of your business.

Addendum: An addition to a contract to describe additional work or changes to the existing agreement.

Advertising: The activity of attracting public attention to your products or services.

After Market: similar to third-party vendors meaning an accessory or attachment made for a tool or product by another manufacturer.

Analyze: to study how best to perform a certain task to maintain safety and avoid injury.

Assembly: The process of putting projects together after all the parts have been cut and sorted.

Assembly Area: The area within your shop that is used to assemble projects.

Backlog: woodwork projects under contract and awaiting completion and delivery to your customers.

Band Saw: a power tool that cuts wood or metal using a blade that is a circular toothed band that is driven by two wheels.

Bank Account: a fund at a bank where you can deposit and withdraw funds.

Belt Sander: a power tool that uses a circular belt with an abrasive grit for sanding surfaces.

Billing: The process of sending an invoice to your customers for services rendered.

Biscuit Joiner: an excellent woodworking tool used for joinery in cabinets and furniture.

Biscuits/Wafers: the compressed beech wafers used in biscuit joinery. They come in three sizes, 20, 10 and 0.

Butt Joints: a joint where one piece of wood is perpendicularly attached to another with no joinery.

Capital: funds available to pay the costs of operating a business.

Carbide Tipped: blades and bits that have carbide attached so they will cut more efficiently and remain sharp longer.

Carpenter: a skilled worker who makes or repairs wooden objects or structures.

Casters: a small wheel attached under a piece of furniture to make it easier to move from one location to another.

Circular Saw: a power saw consisting of a toothed disk rotating at high speed for cutting wood.

Clamps: metal or wooden instruments used to hold wooden parts in place or together while the glue dries.

Collection: obtaining payment for your work.

Communication Skills: the ability to convey your point regarding your work clearly and concisely to facilitate selling woodwork projects.

Competent: sufficiently qualified to perform the work required.

Complaints: an expression of dissatisfaction with something.

Components: The parts of a woodwork projects.

Compressor: a device that compresses air for use with pneumatic tools.

Consumer Tools: tools that are manufactured to lesser standards because of lighter use by non-professionals.

Contract: an agreement between two or more parties to ensure completion of a project and payment for the work.

Creativity: the ability to be original and to develop new ideas using older ideas as a basis or starting point.

Crosscut Jig: an attachment for the table saw that facilitates crosscutting.

Crosscutting: cutting lumber across the grain.

Crown Molding: a decorative molding that is usually applied at the top of a wall against the ceiling.

Custom Cabinets: cabinets that are designed and built for a specific job or location.

Custom Furniture: furniture that is designed and built for a specific customer.

Customer: an individual or company that purchases your products or services.

Cut List: a detailed list of the sizes of all the parts for a specific project.

Cutting Area: the area within a shop that is used for cutting cabinet or furniture parts.

Dados: a rectangular groove cut into a board where a perpendicular board or shelf can be fitted.

Deed Restrictions: a clause in a warranty deed that prohibits certain actions such as conducting business on residential property.

Deft: a manufacturer of excellent clear finishing products such as Deft Clear Wood Finish and Wood Armor.

Deposit: to put money into a bank or other depository.

Depreciation: a loss in value due to age or wear.

Design: to plan out cabinets or furniture.

Design Features: details created to improve the appearance of furniture.

Dovetails: a fan-shaped tenon that forms an interlocking joint.

Dowels: a round wood pin that fits tightly into a corresponding hole to fasten or align an adjacent board.

Drawings: line sketches that clearly describe the construction details for a cabinet or piece of furniture.

Drill: a power tool for drilling holes in wood or metal.

Drill Press: a tabletop or floor mounted drill

Employee: a person who works for you in return for financial or other compensation.

Expansion: the growth of your business to the point that additional employees are needed to operate.

Expenses: costs associated with running your business.

Expert: a person with a high degree of skill or knowledge on a particular subject.

Fingerjoints: interlocking straight tenon joints for assembly of wooden projects.

Finish Sander: a vibrating power sander used for the final sanding of a project.

Finishing: the process of applying a clear or painted coating to a project.

Finishing Area: the area within your shop used to finish projects.

Furniture: articles in a home or office used for living and working comfortably.

Gel Varnish: a clear coat finishing product in gel form instead of liquid.

General Contractor: a person who supervises the activities of everyone working on a construction project.

Gross Income: the total income received from your business activities before expenses are deducted.

Hand Tools: tools that do not require electrical power and used by individuals for various kinds of work

Hardwood Plywood: a multi-layered wood product usually manufactured with layers of hardwoods.

Hardwoods: the hard-to-cut woods of broad-leaved trees.

Health Care: the insurance and facilities required to maintain the health of individuals.

Hourly Rate: the amount per hour paid to employees.

HVLP Spray Equipment: high-volume low-pressure spray equipment used mostly to spray finish on wooden projects.

Income Tax: the tax required by government from every citizen based on the amount of income they make.

Installation: the procedure of installing a cabinet in a home or building.

Insurance: a contract by a party indemnifying another against a specified loss.

IRS: Internal Revenue Service collects income taxes.

Joinery: various methods of strongly fastening wooden parts together.

Lacquer: an excellent clear finish product requiring a respirator to avoid exposure to vapors.

Lacquer Thinner: a liquid used to clean surfaces of lacquer and to thin lacquer.

Learning: the process of acquiring knowledge about certain skills.

License: an authorization from a government body allowing you to perform some form of business.

Maintenance: keeping tools and buildings in good repair.

Materials: products used to build projects.

MDF: medium density fiberboard sheet goods used to build cabinets and furniture.

Measurements: the dimensions of a specific project used to cut the parts.

MinWax: a brand of finishing products including stains and polycrylics.

Modules: small components of a wood project assembled on site.

Mortise and Tenon: an excellent and complex joinery method for wood.

Nails: a pointed piece of metal pounded into wood as a fastener.

Net Income: the income left over after all expenses are deducted from the gross income of a business.

Occupational License: an authorization to participate in a certain occupation or business activity.

Online Banking: conducting your banking using the Internet.

Onsite: doing work at the site of the job instead of at a shop.

Ordinances: laws that apply to various aspects of your work activities.

Overhead: the cost of operating a business.

Paint Thinner: a liquid used to clean or thin paint.

Payroll: salary paid to individuals for work performed.

Payroll Taxes: taxes deducted from individuals for payment to the IRS.

Penalties: fees charged for not adhering to regulations.

Pneumatic Nailer: a pneumatic tool that drives nails into wood.

Polycrylic: a clear finish for wood.

Polyurethane: a clear finish for wood.

Pre-stain: a liquid that partially seals wood surfaces to reduce splotching when stains are applied.

Professional: a person engaged in a certain activity for their livelihood.

Profit: what is left after all operating expenses are deducted from gross income.

Project: a specific job involving one or more products.

Radial Arm Saw: a power saw with a sliding track.

Random Orbit Sander: a power sander that rotates and orbits to sand rapidly without creating circular marks on a wood surface.

Reserve Fund: money set aside for one or more specific purposes.

Reveals: a decorative feature on a cabinet or piece of furniture.

Rip Fence: a straight edge or bar used to guide wood during the ripping process.

Ripping: the process of cutting wood into strips of various width.

Router: a power tool with a sharp bit used to cut grooves and decorative edges.

Saber Saw: a power saw used to cut various radius and cutouts on wood.

Safety: steps taken to remain free from danger, risk or injury.

Salary: compensation paid to an individual for services rendered.

Sanding: the process of smoothing wood in preparation for finishing.

Sanding Belts: circular sanding strips used on belt sanders to sand wood.

Sandpaper: abrasive sheets used to smooth wood surfaces.

Saw horses: four-legged supports to raise work from floor level.

Screws: a metal pin with incised threads used as fasteners.

Security: the idea or concern of being secure.

Self-Employed: working for yourself in a small business.

Self-Analyses: a critical look at yourself and your life.

Self-disciplined: being able to perform required tasks without having someone to make certain things are done.

Self-motivated: being a self-starter who does not require an external motivating force.

Shop: a work area for building wood products.

Shop Layout: a plan for an efficient work area.

Shop Space: the space used for the building of wood products.

Simple Methods: more efficient ways of performing tasks.

Simplified Methods: simpler ways to perform various tasks.

Sliding Compound Miter Saw: a miter saws that facilitate compound cuts and slides to allow for cutting through wide boards.

Small Business: varying definitions exist but basically it is a business that is not considered large.

Social Security: a fund that individuals pay into to have funds available for retirement.

Specifications: details that describe the specifics of a job or project.

Splotching: discoloration of stains that are applied without a pre-stain.

Spray Gun: a tool used to apply finishes by spraying them on the surface.

Stain: a penetrating liquid used to color wood.

Stationary Tools: floor standing power tools intended to remain in one location.

Subcontractor: a self-employed individual who works on a project or projects for the individual who is running the project.

Supply and Demand: the process of setting prices on products based on the demand for it.

Table Saw: a stationary power saw used to rip and crosscut lumber and plywood.

Thickness Planer: a power tool used to reduce the thickness of and smooth wood surfaces.

Trade Tools: tools manufactured for professionals in various fields.

Traditional Methods: precise woodworking methods that may be replaced with simplified methods for faster production of some jobs.

Varnish: a clear coat liquid for finishing.

Visualize: to study the steps involved in safely cutting a board or sheet of plywood.

Wages: hourly fee paid to employees.

Waste Factor: the amount of material that must be calculated in a job because it will be wasted during the cutting.

Index

Income Taxes, 74
increase profits, 15
inexpensive, 132
inexpensive blades, 41
install, 15
install furniture, 110
installments, 74
instructions, 29
insurance, 87
interior space, 47
Internal Revenue Service, 72
Internet, 32, 78
Internet connections, 73
inventory, 12
investment, 11
invoice creation program, 74
invoices, 73
invoicing, 73
ip saw, 36
IRS, 13, 72
IRS regulations, 15

J

Jack Plane, 61
jamb, 27
Jet, 43
jig saw, 36
jigs, 118
job specifications, 146
joinery, 37
joinery tool, 123

K

Keep Learning, 28
keeping customers, 14

Keeping Customers, 78
kickbacks, 118
kitchen cabinet, 20
kitchen cabinets, 25
knives, 59
Knives, 61
Know your limitations, 153

L

lacquer finishes, 116
lacquer thinner, 113
lag bolts, 34
laminate clad, 38
large corporations, 99
large drawers, 130
large job, 143
laundry cabinet, 140
laundry rooms, 140
Lead The Field, 151
Learning, 26
learning new things, 28
letterhead, 144
level of competence, 25
level of expertise, 14
Levels, 61
liability, 87
licensing, 13
listening, 95
local laws, 66
local store, 34
local stores, 32
long grain, 109
long leaf pine, 137
lose money, 14
love for woodworking, 11
low risk, 105

Disclaimer

Everything described in this book is based on my personal experience. Over the years I have gained much experience in the woodworking business and am a competent, though not extraordinary, businessperson. Anyone with good woodworking skills and a sincere desire to learn may be able to attain similar results if he or she puts in the effort. Nevertheless, no guarantees are expressed or implied regarding your own results using the information in this book.

Some individuals are more apt to profit from woodworking than others due to the level of their skills, business acumen, and communication abilities. Regardless of my experience over the years, I can't guarantee that you will succeed in this or any business.

Business of any kind involves the risk of loss, including, but not necessarily limited to, money, time, and energy. In addition to the financial and time considerations, woodworking involves the use of an extensive collection of tools that are capable of inflicting serious injuries.

I have made every effort to accurately describe my experiences in detail, including safety considerations with various power tools, but cannot be held liable for any damages or injuries that may result from the use of this information – even if the user informs me prior to or after these damages or injuries occur.

This book includes the names of and information about several brand name products. Many of these are products I have personally used and others have been highly recommended to me. I own no interest in any of the manufacturers or distributors of these products nor have I received any payment for listing them in this book.

The user of this information agrees that he or she is solely responsible for the consequences of using any tools or products described in this book. It is also the user's responsibility to conduct a reasonable level of due diligence before making any business or legal decisions. The information contained and distributed in this book is not intended as nor should it be considered professional, business, or legal advice.

For any questions please contact bill@positive-imaging.com

About A. William Benitez

Beginning at age twelve, I spent my summers and weekends working with my dad, a general contractor, building homes and commercial buildings. By the time I graduated from high school I was an excellent carpenter. I became a licensed contractor and contracted my first home at age nineteen and followed that by building my own home by age twenty. For more than 40 years I have operated one-person businesses.

Twelve Years with government programs

Twelve years of my life were spent working for local government running federally-assisted housing programs. I started as an inspector with a three-month assignment and was Director of Community Improvement with seventy-eight employees when I resigned twelve years later to do writing and consulting full-time. Because of my extensive experience in housing rehabilitation, I was invited to testify before the Housing Subcommittee of the United States Congress on housing issues.

Writing, Publishing and Consulting

Rehab Notes Library was my publishing company and we published a monthly newsletter (Rehab Notes) with subscribers in all 50 states, Canada and England. I also did consulting and public speaking for agencies and organizations in cities across the country.

Because of my efforts, several community housing programs developed valuable partnerships with local banks to multiply their federal funding.

It was during this period that the National Association of Housing and Redevelopment Officials published my first book about housing rehabilitation. After that I wrote and published eight more guidebooks on various aspects of that subject. I continued writing and consulting until 1980 when the housing assistance programs were cut. After that, I took advantage of my construction experience and started a woodworking business.

Over Twenty Years of Woodworking

For over twenty years, first in Tampa, Florida and then in Austin, Texas, I built hundreds of small and large projects for individuals, companies, churches, and government agencies. During these years I began writing about my experiences and sharing them with other woodworkers.

I published a book and project newsletters on woodworking. My first woodworking book was "SIMPLIFIED WOODWORKING I: A Business Guide For Woodworkers." The monthly project newsletter was called "SIMPLIFIED WOODWORKING" and I wrote and published it for two years.

For a year I performed power tool demonstrations for the Skil Power Tool Company in home improvement stores around Texas. After many years of self employment, I encapsulated my experiences in "THE SELF EMPLOYMENT SURVIVAL MANUAL: How to Start and Operate a One-Person Business Successfully."

I wrote and published several books and ebooks including, "Starting and Operating A Woodworking Business," "Simplified Woodworking Methods and Projects," and, "The Handyman's Guide To Profit: Using Your Skills To Make Money In Any Economy."

Computer Experience

My computer experience dates back more ten years. After a couple of bad experiences with on-site technical support, I began working on my own computers. Since then I have taken many courses on computer repairing, upgrading, troubleshooting and building. I have also taken courses on networking and compiled an extensive library on these subjects. I upgraded and built many computers and acquired A+ Certification and my MCSE (Microsoft Certified Systems Engineer) Certification.

I was born and raised in Tampa, Florida and moved to Austin, Texas in 1986, where I now live with my wife, Barbara Frances. We have three adult children and eight grandchildren.

Other Books

Published By Positive Imaging, LLC

Starting and Operating A Woodworking Business
How To Make Money With Your Skills
by A. William Benitez
http://startingawoodworkingbusiness.com

The Handyman's Guide To Profit:
Using Your Skills To Make Money In Any Economy
By A. William Benitez
http://handyman-business-guide.com

Lottie's Adventure:
A Kidnapping Unraveled
by Barbara Frances
http://lottiesadventure.com

Peace And Healing For The World Using Altars
by Lucretia Jones and Gaila Slaughter
http://peaceandhealingfortheworld.com

The End Of All Worries: We Are All One
by Irie Glajar
http://the-end-of-all-worries.com

12452987R00109

Made in the USA
Lexington, KY
15 December 2011